PUTTING YOUR MONEY TO WORK

PUTTING YOUR MONEY TO WORK

A practical guide to investment and saving

Alan & Deborah Fowler

Sphere Reference

Sphere Reference
27 Wrights Lane, London W8 5SW

First published 1986

Copyright © 1986 Shepherd's Keep Studio Ltd

Printed and bound in Great Britain by
Collins, Glasgow

CONTENTS

INTRODUCTION

'I can't do it, I simply can't,' I insisted. 'You're the one who knows about investment and saving, you're the accountant. This is one book you should write alone.'

'You are so wrong,' Alan replied . . .

And so we went on until late into the night, arguing the pros and cons of my being involved in the writing of this book. We have written a number together, it works well for us and we enjoy it, but this was something different.

'Look,' I said at last, exasperated, 'don't you see, I have absolutely nothing to contribute – I enjoy spending my money too much, I've never had anything to spare to invest or save.'

'Precisely,' Alan replied. 'Your contribution is the most vital of all – *total ignorance.*'

Of course, he was right and, albeit reluctantly, eventually I had to admit it. I was essentially a non-believer. With the exception of property, I saw investment, and certainly savings, as something that belonged to a bygone age; in this consumer society, I believed, if one had it, one spent it. Not so now. The research into this book has opened up a whole new world to me, and my contribution has been to query and question each of Alan's statements until I fully understood them. Given the circumstances, it is amazing we still have a marriage!

The result is a book that really does have something for everyone. For first-timers, like me, who may have as little as £10 a month that can be set aside, or perhaps have inherited a large lump sum on the death of, say, a parent. And also for established investors, like Alan, who perhaps are not entirely satisfied with the advice being given to them by their brokers, and who may wish to have a better understanding of the total market so that they can assess the worth of the advice they are being given.

This, then, is the object of this book – we are looking at the whole investment-and-savings picture with fresh eyes. We have no inbuilt prejudices – our sole aim is to ensure that you, the reader, receive the maximum benefit from *putting your money to work*.

Deborah Fowler

Section 1　Where Are You, and Where Do You Want to Go?

Before you can even contemplate any form of investment plan, you must first have a real understanding of your exact position. The choice of potential investments is bewildering, to say the least, and before you can consider that choice, you need to be very secure in your understanding of your own particular position – not only currently, but what your aims are for the future.

We see this self-analysis as being influenced by three major factors, which we call *The Three Ts*:

TIME

TAX

TEMPERAMENT

Time of course, is a major influencing factor when it comes to considering investment, depending on whether you have your whole working life ahead of you or, for example, are just coming up to retirement. The time of life you have reached will influence whether you want the benefit of income now, accrued income or capital growth.

Tax plays a vital role. Your major concern must be your net position after tax, and any scheme on which you embark must be looked at against the background of its tax-effectiveness.

And *temperament*? Certain types of investment suit certain types of people. You may feel comfortable with a scheme that is going to act as a safety net, to give you security for the future; or you may be the type of person who adores a gamble and is attracted by the potentially lucrative but highly speculative investment.

In the first section of this book, we will be demonstrating how to conduct a complete and thorough assessment of your personal circumstances, to provide the background against which you can measure all investment and savings opportunities.

1 What are your personal circumstances?

There has to be a starting point in any plan, and in the case of investment and saving, that starting point is *you* – you and your personal circumstances. As we see it, self-analysis for this purpose can be divided into five distinct categories:

- Age
- Aspirations/lifestyle
- Employment status
- Relationships
- Location

Let's look at these categories in more detail.

Age

The point you have reached in your life has to be the principal governing factor when it comes to assessing how your money should be made to work for you. Using an adaptation of Shakespeare's 'Seven Ages of Man', the following is how the passing of the years is likely to affect your thinking.

Infant

If a baby is the recipient of some form of inheritance, then it is likely that, in investment terms, the thinking will be geared to long-term planning – investing for the future. Provided that the source of income is not generated by the baby's parents, then

5

the infant, like any other person, is entitled to a personal tax allowance. This factor should greatly influence the nature of the investment – for example, bank and building society investment produces only taxed income, so it would be far better to look at, say, National Savings certificates, which are not taxed at source.

School-age child

By the time children are of school age, parents will have a better idea as to their likely aspirations. Would their children benefit from a private education? Are they the type of person who could handle sensibly the inheritance of a nest egg at, say, eighteen – or would twenty-five be better? A basic decision will need to be made here as to whether the investment is required to produce income for current support – education, clothing, a generally better standard of living – or whether money should be invested on a long-term basis, ultimately to provide that first car, a skiing holiday or a deposit towards the purchase of a first home.

Young single person

Neither investment nor saving is likely to prove particularly attractive to the young single person, whose priority tends to be to earn as much disposable income as possible – and then dispose of it! At this stage in life, pension schemes seem entirely irrelevant, and there is rarely enough money around, nor indeed the inclination, to invest in the stock market. The exception to this, of course, is saving towards the purchase of a

first home. This makes building society and bank special savings accounts very attractive as, undoubtedly, a track record of saving will influence the ease with which a mortgage can be obtained. The only other likely savings will be something set up during childhood, either in the form of National Savings certificates or possibly a National Savings account.

Newly-weds

When a young couple set up home together, their main aim is the acquisition of possessions. The ultimate possession, of course, is their own home – when they can afford to make such a commitment – but this is also the stage at which they will acquire 'things': a three-piece suite, glass, tableware, perhaps the odd antique. They are concerned with feathering their nest, and what better form of investment at this particular age than to collect objects that will give many years' service and, in some

7

cases, will actually increase in value as well? While the couple is generating two incomes this is also a time for living well (e.g. holidays, eating out) while they still have the freedom to enjoy it.

Young family

With the arrival of the first baby, lives and priorities are turned upside down. The emphasis shifts dramatically – suddenly the main criterion is security: life assurance, provision for school fees and medical schemes . . . everything that can be done to keep this new family safe, whatever happens. This is a testing time involving the maximum of stress. The wife will have given up her job, or someone will be paid to look after the children. The husband will be working to establish his career. The flat that suited them well before the baby arrived will be too small. There will be such requirements as a bigger mortgage, more furniture, a spin dryer as well as a washing machine . . . This is the period when there is the maximum pressure on cash, yet it is also the time when plans should be made for the future. Decisions taken now are likely to influence the rest of the family's life.

Alone again

The children are flying the nest, the husband, probably, at the zenith of his career, the wife is, perhaps, providing a second income again. The pressure is off. Now the husband and wife have a chance to be a little selfish. They now become the priority, not their children, and here they are immediately thrown into conflict: on the one hand, they need to provide for old age; on the other, without the children, they have the freedom to enjoy again the relatively high standard of living of their early married life. There is a conflict, too, as to the type of investment. This may well be the time for dabbling in the stock market, yet equally they should perhaps be reviewing their pension schemes, or looking at a personal equity plan.

Retirement

With retirement, there normally comes a dramatic change in the tax position, which in turn can greatly affect investment thinking. Before retirement, when income was relatively high, investment could be looked on as a means of saving. Now, suddenly, there is a requirement for additional income – an investment on which it is necessary to see a return *now*. This is a time for moving to a smaller residence and using the cash so generated for, say, buying an annuity. It is also a time to consider other people's futures – perhaps setting up a covenant to support the education of a talented grandchild and, of course, there is the question of inheritance.

So, age is the major governing factor in determining the types of investments and savings you make, but it is by no means the only consideration.

Aspirations/lifestyle

For some people, investment has one function and one function only – to provide a safety net, security for the future in case things go wrong. For others, investment is a means of generating income to provide a better time, a better standard of living, security playing a very minor role. As we have already demonstrated, this attitude is likely to change according to the stage in life you have reached, but your basic attitude to living needs to be taken into account as well.

Some people are never satisfied – they always want a bigger house, a bigger car, more exotic holidays. Others quite quickly reach their goal as to what they consider to be a comfortable standard of living, and have few, if any, further ambitions. There are people who are supremely indifferent to their surroundings, but spend a fortune on holidays. You may lavish money on your hobby, your children, your pets, food, drink, entertaining, or you may enjoy living frugally and hoarding a large percentage of what you earn. Let's assume that you and your neighbour are earning the same salary, have the same commitments and have decided to put aside the same amount for investment each month. One of you may put your money into National Savings certificates, the other into Georgian silver. Neither of these investments is wrong, just different, reflecting the fact that you and your neighbour are different.

In general terms, therefore, when considering the type of investment you should be making, you need to look at the type of person you are, what interests you, what you expect from life and what your money can do to help you achieve your ambitions.

Employment status

Consider the categories associated with work: there is the employed person, the self-employed, the unemployed and the professional person, working perhaps in a small partnership. The attitude towards investment of, say, an actor who spends nine months of the year out of work and three months earning a great deal of money will vary enormously from someone in full-time employment, earning a steady income. The actor might well owe his sanity to the fact that he keeps busy during his nine months' unemployment by buying and selling antiques or paintings. This would not just provide him with extra income; it would also keep him active, out of the pub and emotionally intact to cope with job opportunities when they arise. A fully employed person simply would not be able to devote enough time to such an additional enterprise.

Self-employed people will naturally be anxious about their pensions, professional people concerned by their possible loss of skill, employed people worried that they will lose their jobs – and all these factors will greatly influence investment decisions.

Relationships

Single, married, widowed or divorced are four possible permutations of personal status. Other permutations include the single parent, the disabled person, the dependent relative, assumed responsibilities towards stepchildren – an endless string of interweaving relationships. These, of course, only reflect personal life – there are also business relationships to consider. We recently met a married couple at a party, who also happened to be partners in a public relations company. They were the first to admit that, painful though it would be financially, they could afford to divorce – but they could *never* afford to break their business partnership.

In assessing any investment or saving scheme, you need to consider your relationships, not just now, but what is likely to happen in the future. Rather than tie up cash in a long-term investment, should you perhaps be building the granny flat that

you know your mother will need sometime during the next five years? Be realistic. Do you need to recognize that your daughter's marriage is on the rocks and she is almost certainly going to look to you for help for herself and her two children? Have you faced the fact that your son is an eternal student, that your spouse's arthritis means that employment for another year or two is the very most that can be expected? Certainly, you cannot go through life trying to anticipate everything that might go wrong, but similarly, you do need to recognize your potential vulnerabilities, and these, usually, are connected with relationships.

Location

Location can have a surprising effect on investment potential. Obviously, if you are working or living abroad, the whole pattern of your thinking will be geared to whether you have residence status in this country or not, and how, as a result, your tax is assessed. However, without moving outside the UK, your location can prove very influential with regard to your investment decisions. Let us give you an example.

We have some charming friends, Anna and James, whose

home always make one feel extraordinarily uncomfortable. You know the sort of thing – more of a show house than a home, exquisitely and expensively furnished, so that you are constantly afraid of relaxing in case you make something dirty or drop or spill anything. About five years ago, James was posted to Bradford. Having sold their house in Richmond (in Surrey), they found that the kind of house they could afford to buy in West Yorkshire was vastly bigger and better than anything they could have contemplated in London. They bought an enormous manor house just outside Skipton, and Anna set about her usual task of turning it into a dream home. It was a mammoth job, as you can imagine, but in her inimitable way, she succeeded. However, two years later, James was moved south again, and so they put the house up for sale, confident of making an absolute killing, bearing in mind the improvements they had made. Their investment proved to be a disaster: the kind of sophisticated elegance that would have greatly enhanced, say, a Knightsbridge flat was hardly appropriate in an enormous Yorkshire country house, and the price they had to ask to recoup their expenditure was way over market value. In the end, it took them two years to sell the house, during which time they carried the burden of two mortgages, and they were finally forced to sell it for nearly £20,000 less than they had originally anticipated.

This example demonstrates the fact that investment in your home, despite dramatic increases in property values, is not entirely foolproof, and certainly your location should play a part in your overall investment thinking. Home is so important to us. In the right environment we work better, play better and our relationships are better. Since, for most people, buying a house is the major investment of their lives, any change in its status is going to completely alter their overall investment plan. Look at where you want to be in ten years' time. Do you want a larger house for your increasing family, a house in the country instead of the town, a holiday home as well as your main dwelling place, or are you looking for somewhere smaller now that your children are off your hands? Do give very careful thought to this, for it should represent the nucleus round which the rest of your investment planning is geared.

In the next chapter, we will be looking in detail at how to analyse your personal circumstances. Here we are asking to look at your life, purely in general terms – what you have now and what you hope to achieve in the future. Do discuss your basic objectives with other members of your family; a fresh view is always valuable. Also bear in mind that, whatever form of investment you adopt, chopping and changing your plan is bound to cost you money, so you do need to be very sure that the decision you take is the right one.

2   A personal audit

What details do you require in order to undertake a personal audit? Your ultimate aim should be to find out what you are worth: what your net income is now and in the future, and therefore what your net worth is likely to be in, say, five and ten years' time. This is not something you can calculate on the back of an envelope, however simple you may believe your financial affairs to be. We thought it would be helpful to compile a questionnaire for you to fill in, which will detail all the information that you will require to make a sensible assessment for your future investment and saving plans. Head the questionnaire with the name(s) of yourself and your spouse (if applicable) and then answer the following questions.

Personal details

Date of birth: (a) of yourself   (b) of your spouse
Occupation: (a) of yourself   (b) of your spouse
Retirement age: (a) of yourself   (b) of your spouse
Are you and your spouse in good health? Be honest here – do not be pessimistic, but if one of you is in poor health, have the courage to say so. Once you have written down the details, you will find it easier to think positively about taking this fact into consideration in your future planning.

Family details

List the names of your children, their ages, whether they are married, single, divorced or widowed. Also list the names and ages of your grandchildren. Are any of your children, or grandchildren, likely to change their status – i.e. are they about to marry or divorce, or are they likely to come up against any problem that will involve additional financial support?

Your aim

Here you need to decide precisely what you are trying to achieve:

- Do you wish to increase the value of your assets?
- Do you wish to increase your net income?
- Do you wish to improve or provide for a pension?
- Do you wish to reduce your tax liabilities – i.e. your potential Capital Gains Tax or Inheritance Tax?
- Do you wish to make special provision for a dependant?
- Have you any other specific requirements?

Assets

You should now make a detailed list of your assets, subdivided under your name and that of your spouse:

- House
- Additional properties
- Investments
  - Building society accounts
  - Bank deposit/current accounts
  - National Savings
  - Equities
  - Fixed-interest investments
  - Unit trusts
  - Guaranteed income bonds/guaranteed growth bonds
  - Investment bonds

- Investment in private companies
- Share of business/partnerships
● Personal goods – e.g. cars, boats, caravans, jewellery, domestic items, antiques, paintings – indeed, anything you own that has a saleable value

Take time with this assessment. We are inclined to take so many of our possessions for granted, without really appreciating their full worth. List everything, *absolutely everything*, that could be described as an asset.

Income

Here, state gross income rather than net, since a net assessment can be made at the end of the questionnaire. Again, list income separately, under your name and that of your spouse.

- *Earned income*
  - Salary
  - Business profits/share
  - Private pension
  - State pension
  - Freelance/casual work
- *Unearned income*
  - Building society interest (grossed up)
  - Bank deposits (grossed up)
  - National Savings
  - Trust income
  - Equities
  - Fixed-interest investments
  - Unit trusts
  - Annuity and bond income: taxable and non-taxable
  - Private company investments
  - Any other sources of unearned income

Liabilities

This again should be subdivided between yourself and your spouse.

- Mortgages on private residence
- Mortgages on any other property
- Bank overdraft
- Bank loan accounts

- Other loans, including any outstanding balances with credit card companies
- Taxation
- Any requirement for immediate capital expenditure

Expenditure

- Mortgage interest
- Bank interest on any overdrafts or loan accounts
- Day-to-day living costs
- Holidays
- Insurance premiums
- Education
- Gifts
- Covenants
- Any other form of committed expenditure

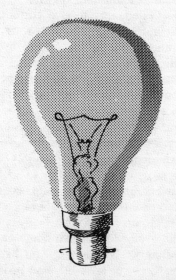

Of course, in this questionnaire, there may be some element of expenditure, income, asset or liability that we have not mentioned but which is specific to you. In this respect, it is vital that you make sure you write down every single item, however

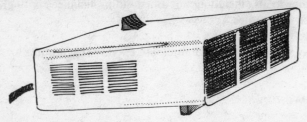

trivial it may seem – after all, that £10 worth of premium bonds could bring you £100,000 next week – so don't forget to include it!

Having satisfied yourself that you have remembered everything, first summarize all your assets at their current value, and total them. Then repeat the exercise for your total liabilities. Deduct these from your assets and you will achieve a figure of net asset value – perhaps better described simply as *total wealth*. Then summarize your income and expenditure position, again with the objective of establishing your net income.

These figures will demonstrate your current position, which will either prove comforting or extremely worrying! Either way, do not be tempted to juggle the figures around. You may consider it justified to mislead other people as to your exact position, but you cannot afford to mislead yourself.

Having set your benchmark, now is the time to look to the future. Using these figures as a basis, you should try to assess how you see your position developing. It is difficult to generalize in terms of how many years ahead you should work, because so much depends on the stability of your circumstances. However, it would be useful to look at your likely position in five and in ten years' time, and here there are certain factors you should take into account. For example, are you, or your spouse, likely to inherit or receive any material gifts? Are any of your children liable to leave home and cease to be a financial responsibility? Is either of you likely to receive a substantial increase or suffer a decrease in income? Is there going to be any large decrease in expenditure – e.g. the paying off of a mortgage, a loan, an overdraft? Are you just about to take on an increased liability – a bigger home, a second home, school fees? And finally, without doubt the most difficult question of them all: can you make a sensible appraisal of your own and your spouse's life expectancy, given a fair wind?

Ideally, you should end up with two sheets of paper – one showing your assets and liabilities today, in five years' time and in ten years' time, and the other showing your income and expenditure today, in five years' time and in ten years' time. This will show you precisely what you have to play with both in an income and in a capital sense. However, before you can start to plan any investment or savings programme, there is one other major factor that has to be taken into account – *tax*.

3   The influence of tax

Tax, inevitably, must greatly influence your current and future financial position, and therefore must also affect the direction of your investment policy. While the tax-effectiveness of any plan is only one consideration, it is, without doubt, the most important.

Take an obvious example: if you are paying tax at 60 per cent on the top slice of your income, your investments should be directed towards long-term growth and capital profit, which is

taxable at no more than 30 per cent. What you want to avoid is an investment that is going to produce a high yield, which will only exacerbate your tax burden. Conversely, if you are retired with an income below the level of the age allowance, your nest egg should not be on deposit with a bank or building society because interest is paid to you net of tax and you cannot reclaim the tax deducted. Instead, you should be looking for an investment with a high yield, paid to you gross.

Before you can plan your affairs effectively, therefore, you do need a basic understanding of the tax structure. For ease of reference, we felt it sensible here to set out the full details of the three taxes that can affect your personal wealth and income – *income tax, Capital Gains Tax* and *Inheritance Tax*.

Income tax

Income tax allowances

Everyone can enjoy income that is free of income tax up to the level of personal allowance to which they are entitled. The main personal allowances for 1986/87 are:

Personal allowance	–	single person	£2335
	–	married couple	£3655
Age allowance (where either spouse is over sixty-five)	–	single person	£2850
	–	married couple	£4505
Wife's earned-income allowance (where both husband and wife are earning)	–		£2335

The age allowance is a substitute for the personal allowance, if either you or your spouse is over sixty-five – it is *not* an additional allowance. It is also reduced if your income (or joint income, in the case of a husband and wife) exceeds £9400 – in fact, it is actually reduced by two-thirds of any income above £9400 until the allowance equals the standard personal allowance. This means that the age allowance ceases to be of any benefit to a married couple with an income of £10,675, or a single person with an income of £10,173.

All these allowances are adjusted annually in the Budget, to keep pace with inflation.

Other allowable costs

A number of costs can be offset against income – in other words, deducted from gross income to arrive at the net amount that is subject to tax. Your personal affairs should be organized to take maximum advantage of these allowances. These are the main allowable costs:

- Interest paid on mortgages or loans to purchase, or improve, a property that is your only or main residence. You will be entitled to tax relief, on a loan or loans up to £30,000.
- Interest paid on mortgages or loans to purchase, or improve, a property that is available for letting throughout the year, and is actually let for at least 26 weeks each year.
- Interest paid on money borrowed to provide capital or loan finance for your own business, or for a trading company in which you control at least 5 per cent of the equity.
- Investments under the Business Expansion Scheme, up to £40,000 in any tax year (*see* pp. 73–4 for full details of this).
- Pension premiums paid into an approved scheme if you are employed, or on a personal pension policy if you are in now pensionable employment or are self- employed (*see* Chapter 13 for full details).
- Expenses necessarily incurred in carrying out your work – e.g. travel, meals, hotels. Two areas that are quite specifically not allowable are travel between home and work, and entertaining.
- Any fees or subscriptions payable to professional bodies relevant to your working life.
- If you are trading on your own account or in partnership, all appropriate costs, overheads and expenses specifically relevant to your business activities.
- Deeds of covenant, and payment of alimony or maintenance under a court order or decree.

So many people do not take full advantage of these allowable costs. Do check your outgoings very carefully and make sure

you have included every possible item of expense on your tax
return.

Rates of income tax

Rates of tax for 1986/87 on taxable income are:

Basic rate on first £17,200	(i.e. £0–17,200)	29%
Higher rate on next £3000	(i.e. £17,201–20,200)	40%
Higher rate on next £5200	(i.e. £20,201–25,400)	45%
Higher rate on next £7900	(i.e. £25,401–33,300)	50%
Higher rate on next £7900	(i.e. £33,301–41,200)	55%
Top rate of tax on income over £41,200		60%

These rates apply to single people, or to the joint income of a
married couple. A wife may elect to be taxed separately from
her husband, but in doing so, her husband will lose the £1320
of his earned-income allowance. This being the case, there is
little point in a wife seeking separate taxation unless both she
and her husband have a fairly high income – it would be an
advantage to be taxed separately if your joint income (before
personal allowances) is over £26,520, of which the wife is
earning at least £6986.

This, then, summarizes the income tax position, and certainly
demonstrates that high-income earners should be looking at
ways of investing their money to increase their capital rather
than their incomes. Conversely, low earners must ensure that
all their investments yield gross income, so that they can take
full advantage of their personal allowance and allowable costs.

Capital Gains Tax

Capital Gains Tax (CGT) is payable at the flat rate of 30 per
cent. It applies to the disposal of all or any of your assets,
including gifts, except for specifically exempted items. Exempted items include:

- The disposal of your only, or main, residence
- Transfers between husband and wife

- Sales of government stocks and certain corporate fixed interest stocks
- Disposals arising from death
- Personal belongings worth £3000 or less at date of disposal, or having a useful life of less than fifty years when you acquired them
- British money
- Gifts to charities and certain national heritage bodies, museums and universities

In addition, there is no Capital Gains Tax levied on the first £6300 (1986/87) of capital gain in any one year, but this exemption cannot be carried forward. In other words, if you made no profit on the disposal of your assets last year, you cannot use that unused exemption allowance because you made £10,000 this year. Losses, however, can be carried forward indefinitely. For example, if last year you sold some shares for £3000 less than the purchase price, you can, at any time in the future, deduct this loss from subsequent gains.

There is a fair amount of rather similar and confusing jargon associated with CGT, and it is worth listing these terms, together with explanations, in order to clarify their use:

Chargeable proceeds   These represent the sale price or disposal value, less any disposal costs – e.g. stockbroker's fee in the case of shares, auctioneer's fee in the case of, say, a painting.

Chargeable gains   This is the term used to describe chargeable proceeds, less allowable costs and indexation allowance (*see below*).

Allowable costs   This is the purchase price, plus any purchase costs and expenditure on the asset since acquisition.

Taxable gains   This is used to describe chargeable gains, less the annual £6300 exemption and any losses brought forward.

Indexation allowance

Indexation of costs is allowed by reference to the retail price index. The indexation rules are complicated, and professional advice is needed in complex situations. However, it is well worth referring to the retail price index, for, although you may have made a profit on the disposal of an asset, it could be that, when inflation is taken into account, no profit has been made at all, or indeed you might even have made a loss. Losses as a result of indexation can be carried forward against future years' profits.

CGT relief

There are several circumstances in which you may be able to qualify for CGT relief. One example is the disposal of business assets and investments in family companies on retirement. CGT may also be deferred when an asset is gifted by an individual or, indeed, a trustee. You have to make a formal claim for what is known as 'roll-over relief' and this claim has to be made jointly by both the donor and the donee. What effectively happens is that the donee takes over the asset at its original cost – in other words, he/she recognizes no increase in value from when the asset was originally purchased. CGT is therefore suspended until the donee disposes of the asset, when he/she will have to pay full CGT on the difference between the original purchase price and the price at which he/she makes his/ her sale.

These fairly arbitrary conditions for CGT demonstrate the need for extreme caution when it comes to realizing investments and savings. Long-term planning can certainly greatly relieve the potential burden of Capital Gains Tax.

Inheritance Tax

This was introduced in the 1986 Budget to take the place of Capital Transfer Tax. No Inheritance Tax is charged on an estate when the total value is less than £71,000, and so, on the face of it, it might appear that, for many people, this tax is not relevant. However, with the continuing spiral in house prices, it is relatively easy to find oneself in a position where one's estate is worth more than this figure and therefore attracts Inheritance Tax.

Inheritance Tax is chargeable at the appropriate full rate on assets transferred at death, and on gifts made within three years of death. Gifts made to individuals between three and seven years prior to death will suffer tax based on the value of the gift at the date it was given, at the scale rate applicable to the estate on death but subject to a tapering percentage relief (more details of this in a moment). The effect of this is that lifetime gifts, made to individuals more than seven years prior to the death of the person making the gift, will be free from Inheritance Tax, although, of course, they may be subject to Capital Gains Tax. Where Capital Gains Tax has been paid on a gift made within seven years prior to death, it does not safeguard the estate from having to pay Inheritance Tax as well, so one does have to be very careful. The exemption of lifetime gifts to individuals over seven years before death, and the tapering relief, can also be applied to the setting up of specific types of trust funds, for the exclusive benefit of, say, a child or perhaps a disabled member of the family. However, in order to attract tax exemption, it is imperative that donors cannot benefit in any way from the trust.

Certain transfers on death, or made immediately prior to death, are exempt from Inheritance Tax. These are:

- All transfers made to the transferor's spouse.
- The first £3000 of chargeable transfers made in a fiscal year.
- Outright gifts of up to £250 to any one person in a year of assessment. If the gifts to one person exceed £250 in a year of assessment commencing after 5 April 1981, the £250 exemption will not be available to set against the first slice of the total gifts to that person. Prior to 6 April 1981, the £250 could be used to exempt the first £250 of gifts of any size during a year of assessment.
- The amount by which the preceding financial year's gifts fell short of the permissible limit of £3000.
- Normal expenditure out of income. The transfer must be normal or regular, and leave the transferor with sufficient income after tax to maintain his or her usual standard of living.
- Gifts in consideration of marriage, to either of the parties of

the marriage, up to the limit of £5000 from parents, £2500 from grandparents and £1000 from any other person.

- Transfers in the course of a trade, provided the transfer is an allowable deduction for tax purposes.
- Certain gifts to charities:
  - Gifts to charities are exempt if made on or after 15 March 1983. If the gifts were made before 15 March 1983 then (a) they are exempt provided that they were made more than one year before death, or (b) the exemption is limited to £250,000 if they were made on or within one year of death.
  - Distribution out of discretionary trusts to charity is exempt.
  - If someone by his/her will settles property on a discretionary trust and, within two years of his/her death, the property is distributed from the trust to a charity, then the property will be exempt on the death as well as on the distribution.
- Unlimited gifts to political parties made more than one year before death. For gifts within one year of death, the limit is £100,000.
- Gifts for national purposes to specified national institutions.
- Gifts for public benefit authorized by the Treasury.
- All assets that pass on the death of a person on active service.
- Death benefits payable to dependants under retirement annuity schemes and occupational pension schemes.

From 18 March 1986 rates of Inheritance Tax on the value of an estate are:

On the first £71,000	(i.e. £0–71,000)	Nil
On the next £24,000	(i.e. £71,001–95,000)	30%
On the next £34,000	(i.e. £95,001–129,000)	35%
On the next £35,000	(i.e. £129,001–164,000)	40%
On the next £42,000	(i.e. £164,001–206,000)	45%
On the next £51,000	(i.e. £206,001–257,000)	50%
On the next £60,000	(i.e. £257,001–317,000)	55%
Over £317,000		60%

The relief applied to lifetime gifts is:

Up to 3 years	prior to death	Nil
3 to 4 years	" "	20%
4 to 5 years	" "	40%
5 to 6 years	" "	60%
6 to 7 years	" "	80%
Over 7 years	" "	100%

Gifts to trusts – other than the two already mentioned concerning children and disabled people – and gifts involving companies are subject to Inheritance Tax. These will be subject to tax at 50% of the full scale rates whenever they are made, and then, if the gift is by an individual, will be brought back into the estate on subsequent death, and the tax recomputed.

As this chapter has demonstrated, the influence of tax on our lives is considerable, and any plan for investment and saving must be geared to do everything possible to relieve the burden imposed by taxation.

We hope that the details outlined above will provide a useful reference point for you as you consider the various investment and saving opportunities we will be discussing in the next section.

Section 2   Surveying What Is Available

Now that you understand yourself, your requirements and your tax position, it is time to look at what the market can offer you. In this section, we will be dealing with all the major investment opportunities, giving details of how they work and how best to approach them, and providing sufficient information and opinion to help you decide whether they are appropriate for you.

Some of these categories may be of no interest to you, but it is worth studying them, even if they do not immediately appeal, because there may be some implication that had not occurred to you and which could well prove useful.

So, let's go window shopping . . .

4   Your home and possessions

Investment in property and chattels has almost certainly proved the most effective way of protecting the purchasing power of money in recent years, as well as providing a reliable hedge against inflation. Let us first look at your home.

Freehold property

The purchase of a freehold property is probably the largest investment that most people ever make in their lifetime. It is also likely to be the best. During the last ten years, the average house price has risen by nearly 250 per cent – a £20,000 house bought in 1976 would fetch £70,000 today. In the last twenty years, the rise has been even more dramatic, representing a 900 per cent increase – a £7000 house purchased in 1966 would thus be worth £70,000 today. Both these examples show an increase of at least 12 per cent per annum, compound, while the retail price index over the same period has increased only 10 per cent per annum compound, as indeed have building costs.

All this is very encouraging. It shows that freehold property is a very good investment in its own right, but it is made even more attractive for the home buyer by mortgage interest relief and Capital Gains Tax exemption. The effect that a house purchase has on personal wealth is quite astounding. Let us look at an example. Let us assume that Joe Bloggs purchased a £7000 house in 1966, with a £5000 endowment mortgage. This meant that his personal equity in the house was £2000 at that time. By now, the same house would be worth £70,000, but Joe's mortgage would have remained the same. Thus his equity would have risen from £2000 to £65,000 – a growth of 19 per cent per annum *free of tax*.

We would suggest that anyone, at any age, cannot fail to benefit from the purchase of a freehold property, provided it is properly surveyed, adequately insured and, if a mortgage is required, you have the necessary income to service that mortgage.

Let us look at the further implications of buying a freehold property.

Interest relief and improvement grants

As we stated in our chapter on tax, you can enjoy mortgage interest relief on your only, or main, residence. This applies not only to the purchase price, but also to home improvements, up to a total borrowing of £30,000. We list below those types of home improvements for which, if money is borrowed to undertake them, you can expect tax relief on the interest paid.

- Home extensions and loft conversions.
- Central and solar heating installations (excluding portable radiators and night storage radiators not fixed to a permanent spur outlet).
- The cost of replacing one form of heating with another – for example, changing from gas to oil.

- Installation of double-glazing even though it is in a detachable form. Replacement of windows and/or doors generally is included.

- Insulation of roof or walls.
- Installation of bathrooms and other similar plumbing.
- Kitchen and bedroom units (e.g. sink units) that are affixed to and become part of the building. In practice, a range of matching units may be treated as qualifying as a whole, even though only some of them qualify; however, cookers, refrigerators and similar appliances are always excluded.
- Connection to mains drainage.
- Cost of erection of garages, garden sheds, greenhouses, patios and fences.
- Re-covering or reconstructing a roof.
- Construction or landscaping of gardens.
- Construction of swimming pools.
- Reconstruction of property – e.g. conversion into flats.
- Underpinning a house.
- Rebuilding a façade.
- Insertion or renewal of damp-proof course. Dry and wet rot treatment.
- Replacement of electrical installations.
- Extensive repointing, pebble-dashing, texture-coating or stone-cladding (but excluding painting).
- Installation of fire or burglar alarms.

- Installation of water-softening equipment forming a permanent part of the plumbing system.
- Construction of driveways and paths.
- Extensive replacement of guttering.

The above list is not exhaustive. In particular, expenditure on a number of smaller items may be met by a combined loan qualifying for relief – for example, improvements under the Clean Air Act, fire-precaution works, installation of water heating and ring mains electricity and the concreting or other improvements of driveways or paths.

Consider, too, the possibility of improvement grants from your local authority. When purchasing a property you may well find that estate agents mention the possibility of an improvement grant in the particulars, and certainly you want to look out for this. Wherever there is a lack of basic amenities – and this does not just mean plumbing; it also means central heating, insulation, etc. – you may well be able to obtain a grant, which, of course, means your investment is being greatly enhanced in value at someone else's expense!

The cost of acquiring a freehold property

Firstly, there is the question of the solicitor's conveyancing fee – and despite recent legislation, we would recommend that you always employ the services of a solicitor for your purchase. Conveyancing fees and charges do have a tendency to vary somewhat, but you should think in terms of between 1 and 2 per cent of the purchase price as being the norm. If you employ a solicitor who is not local to the property, or if the conveyancing is particularly complicated for any reason, these fees can rise dramatically.

In addition to the straightforward conveyancing fees, your solicitor may also charge you extra for acting on your behalf with regard to the negotiation of a mortgage. The bank or building society will also charge you for the cost of their solicitor, acting on their behalf. Again, these figures together are likely to be between 1 and 2 per cent of the purchase price.

You will also have to pay land registration fees and stamp duty:

| Cost of property | Land registration fees | | Stamp duty |
| | 1st registration | Transfer of registration | |
£	£	£	£
10,000	12	15	NIL
20,000	27	40	NIL
50,000	72	115	500
100,000	147	210	1,000
200,000	167	290	2,000
1,000,000	325	680	10,000

Property as investment

So far, we have tended to think of a freeholder as being the owner/
occupier, and as already indicated, you are unlikely to make a
better investment in your life than the purchase of your own
freehold home. However, what advantages are there in purchasing
property as an investment, in addition to your own home? There
are, of course, no tax advantages. The profit you make on buying
and selling property will be subject to Capital Gains Tax. The
income derived from any letting is subject to income tax, and there
is no mortgage relief, unless a commercial rent is obtained for at
least 26 weeks each year and the property is available to be let for
the balance of the year. This in itself, however, does not make the
investment potential unattractive, but you do need to approach the
whole subject with extreme caution.

Until about ten years ago, there were very rich pickings to be
had from property investment, but now, at least in areas of high
demand, the conversion and development of individual properties has been heavily over-subscribed. For example, take the
area in which we ourselves live – Oxfordshire. Virtually all the
picturesque farm labourers' cottages have already been converted, as have any agricultural buildings for which it has been
possible to obtain planning permission for conversion. Now, in
the rare instance when a barn and a piece of adjoining land do
come on the market, the price that is asked is horrific, and
certainly would be only appropriate if you intended to live in
the property yourself, once it was developed.

Let's take the case of a mythical barn, which you are able to purchase for, say, £45,000, but when converted into a four-bedroomed house should sell for at least £100,000. The conversion costs will be between £35,000 and £40,000 and – *bingo!* – suddenly you can see yourself making a cool £15,000–20,000 profit. Unfortunately it is simply not that easy. To spend £85,000 on property in the hopes of making £15,000 is too risky. Assuming you have to borrow at least some of the money, that will set the interest clock ticking. Builders have a reputation for never finishing on time, and in most cases, they live up to that reputation – not necessarily because of their own inefficiency, but simply because of the vagaries of the weather. Then there are the fees and the marketing costs of selling the property, and the fact that, however carefully your architect has calculated the cost of conversion, once the work starts, hidden extras always emerge. The result: a rapidly diminishing profit that could well end up as a loss.

If, however, you were undertaking this conversion for yourself, it would be a different story. Once the building was finished you would be living in it for a number of years, thus putting some distance between the original costs of purchase and conversion and the ultimate selling price when you decide to move – and when you did eventually move, your profits would not be subject to CGT.

These days, clever investment in property development is very largely dependent upon your ability to anticipate trends in property demand. Certainly, if you can acquire property in an area that is 'up and coming', you may well be in a position to make your investment pay. This really is the secret – seeing the potential of something that, in the eyes of the rest of the world, is not yet an attractive proposition. We have a friend who, during the last thirty years, has quite deliberately purchased all the property around his home town which houses sitting tenants – on the face of it, not an attractive proposition. However, gradually, as the sitting tenants die, he has ended up with a vast number of properties for a fraction of their true worth. Of course, with a waiting game such as this, you need both the time and the money available to allow your investment to pay off.

We have looked at property investment largely as it applies to private dwellings, though of course you could invest in commercial property. This, honestly, is not something we would recommend, unless you have some sort of specialist knowledge – i.e. you are a builder or an architect, and so have an additional vested interest in seeing property developed. Certainly buying a little row of shops would be a disaster. Your tenants are likely to come and go at an appalling rate – a high proportion of them going out of business while owing you rent – and indeed, you could find yourself with the property vacant more often than in use. Garages, cinemas and factories should also be avoided – these are single-purpose buildings where your likely return against your risks makes an unsatisfactory investment. Offices are probably the best commercial property investment, since you can spread the risk by letting a number of different types of tenant, and of course the special structural requirements of these buildings are not significant.

In general terms, therefore, be wary of investment in property unless, of course, it is your own home. It is no longer a game for the amateur – you really do need to know what you are doing. Also, do recognise that regular buying and selling will establish, in the eyes of the Inland Revenue, that you are trading. What you thought was a capital profit may be treated as earned income . . !

Leasehold property

A lease is a wasting asset. As every year goes by, so your investment slips away from you, and once the lease is terminated, your asset is gone. In theory, certainly, it is better to pay a premium for a medium- or long-term leasehold property at a low rental than simply rent premises on a month-by-month basis. Hopefully, the premium you pay will at least hold its value, so that, even if you do not make any money out of the buying and selling of the lease, you get your money back if you move well before the lease expires. In some areas of extremely high demand, leasehold property does take on many of the same characteristics as that of freehold. For example, most of central London is leasehold and so much in demand that, if you buy a long lease with, say, sixty years left to run, you can expect to sell it ten years later and still see the kind of increase in value that one would expect from a freehold. Investing in a leasehold property as your dwelling is one thing, but you should be very wary when considering its investment potential beyond that.

Below is a table of stamp duty and land registration fees in respect of leasehold property:

Rent not exceeding (per annum) £	Stamp duty TERM OF LEASE				Land registration fees
	Less than 7 years £	7–35 years £	35–100 years £	Over 100 years £	First registration by original lessee £
500	nil	10	60	120	5
1,000	10	20	120	240	10
5,000	50	100	600	1,200	50
10,000	100	200	1,200	2,400	100

Chattels

By chattels we mean personal possessions, the collection of which is traditionally considered to be a sound investment – e.g.

coins, stamps, paintings, antique furniture, porcelain, jewellery. There is no doubt that this sort of investment brings with it an enormous amount of pleasure, but if you are seriously thinking of putting your money to work, this is not the right answer for you. Acquiring these items is easy, and convincing yourself of their increasing value equally so, but when it comes to their disposal, all too often they fetch only a fraction of what you believe to be their true worth. It also needs to be borne in mind that these items pay no interest – in fact, in many cases, they actually cost money to keep: storage facilities (sometimes at a specific temperature), insurance, the fitting of special locks and burglar alarms and so on.

If you are a *genuine* expert in some particular subject, it may be that you can make money from the buying and selling of chattels, but usually this is best achieved by actually doing something to improve the chattels while they are in your

possession. For example, we have a friend who buys and sells pictures, but she is also a picture framer and much of the money she makes is from the framing service she offers, rather than the buying-and-selling process. If your particular interest is antique clocks, there might well be money to be made out of buying broken, unworkable clocks and restoring them to their former glory. However, in these instances we are not so much talking about an investment than about the running of a small business, which is a different thing altogether.

Chattels do have a big attraction for the high-tax payer, who actively does not want additional income, but it is all too easy to 'catch a cold', for these types of investment are all subject to fashion. People's requirements and standards can change radically over the years, and what you have to ask yourself is whether you can spare the time and, more important, the money to wait until your investment reaches its true potential.

We have a delightful Canadian cousin who, some years ago, decided that money was to be made by investing in a particular type of English china. He has spent an absolute fortune shipping over quantities of the stuff, and his entire house is now a mass of figurines, toby jugs and the like. His wife has taken to keeping the curtains drawn all day since there is no way she can cope with the dusting, and because of these pieces (which he describes in his North American way as 'collectables'), they literally cannot move. Yes, of course his enormous quantity of collectables has increased in value – but by no means, we suspect, than the rate of inflation – and what about disposal? The one thing he has never considered is whether there is a market in Canada for the china he has amassed, and our feeling is that none exists. So what is his solution? His wife, eyeing the gathering dust in despair, suggests a marathon car boot sale. She is probably right.

Invest in chattels for pleasure by all means. If you happen to make money as well, terrific – but do not look on it as a serious form of investment.

The message for this chapter, therefore, is this: the best

investment you are ever likely to make in your life is the purchase of your own freehold home, and the bigger, the better, provided you can service the mortgage. It is the best, the fastest and the surest way of acquiring wealth.

5   The High Street banks

What the major banks can offer you is a secure haven for your savings and a temporary home for your investments during any transition stage, such as reinvestment. It should prove a very satisfactory relationship – you deal direct with the bank, there are no intermediaries, you have easy access to your money and no costs are involved.

Banks are in the very forefront of the international money market, and their interest rates fluctuate accordingly, being constantly reviewed in response to the world economy, oil prices, international diplomatic situation, trade figures and political pressures. Other institutions take their lead from the banks' reactions to these pressures.

There is always intense competition between the banks with regard to their interest rates. This competition extends into the types of services they offer, but looking in general terms at the major High Street banks, there is little to choose between them in terms of the facilities they have available. The rate of interest you will receive on funds deposited with a bank will be determined largely by the current money market. Thereafter, it will be influenced by the amount of money involved, the length of time you are prepared to commit that money, the period of notice of withdrawal and, up to a point, the amount of service the bank will be expected to provide.

In describing the various deposit and saving accounts quoted by the major banks, we feel it would be helpful to give you some sort of indication as to the interest rates on offer. *During the lifetime of this book, interest rates will vary enormously, so we have decided it would be most useful to quote a bank base rate*

from which we will work, which we have set at 11.5 per cent.
This figure and the current market feeling that it will move
lower, have formed the basis of all the yields and interest rates
given throughout this book, whether from banks, saving
accounts or the various other investments we describe in the
chapters ahead. What is important is not the actual rate we
quote, but the relationship between the various types of
schemes on offer. As a quick guide, you should adjust the
figures quoted by the variance between 11.5 per cent and the
base rate existing at the time you read this book, *but always
check the current position as well.*

Each of the banks has its own descriptions for the various
types of deposit accounts, but broadly speaking, they fall into
the following categories.

Ordinary deposit account

This is a very flexible facility. You can put on deposit almost
any sum of money as frequently as you wish, and withdrawals
are easy to make. This account is particularly helpful if your

future planning is somewhat uncertain. It offers you a better rate of interest than an ordinary current account, but places very little restriction on access to your money. Interest rates are:

- Seven days' notice of withdrawal: 5.8% net of tax (7.75% gross)
- Three months' notice of withdrawal: 6.35% net of tax (8.5% gross)

Money market fixed deposit account

This account requires a specific deposit of a minimum of £10,000 for a fixed period, which can be anything from literally overnight to six months or even five years. Typical money market interest rates are:

| | DEPOSIT OF £10,000 | | DEPOSIT OF £100,000 | |
	Net	Gross	Net	Gross
Overnight	7.84%	10.5%	8.4%	11.25%
7 days	7.84%	10.5%	8.3%	11.12%
3 months	7.1%	9.5%	7.6%	10.25%
6 months	7.1%	9.5%	7.6%	10.25%
1 year	7.1%	9.5%	7.6%	10.25%

Money market notice deposit account

This again requires a specific deposit of not less than £10,000, which can be left on deposit for an indefinite period. However, there is an agreed period of withdrawal, which can vary from seven days to three months, six months or even a year or more.

Investment account

This is a variation on the ordinary deposit account, but here, a minimum balance of anything from £1000 to £5000 will be required initially. However, once the account is opened, smaller deposits of, say, £100 will be accepted. Typically, banks require one months' notice of withdrawal. Interest rates do vary slightly from bank to bank, depending upon the minimum deposit and period of notice, but on average, they are:

- One months' notice of withdrawal: 7.1% net of tax (9.5% gross), paid *quarterly*
- One month's notice of withdrawal: 6.9% net of tax (9.25% gross), paid *monthly*

High interest cheque account

This is almost a current account, except that it requires a minimum balance of between £1000 and £5000, and in some instances, there may be limitations on the number and value of cheques that may be drawn. However, cheque cards and overdraft facilities can usually be linked to this type of account, and cash can be withdrawn without notice. No interest is payable when the balance falls below the minimum amount, and typical interest rates are 6.5% net of tax 8.75% gross, paid quarterly.

Interest-earning current account

This is the device used by the major banks to entice new customers. The description of the account varies from bank to bank, as do the precise circumstances that are required before you qualify for interest on what is virtually a normal current account. In all cases, the interest offered is fairly low and is linked to the maintenance of a minimum balance during a monthly or quarterly period. There are occasionally some restrictions as to the services available, but most banking facilities are linked to these accounts. Typical interest rates are:

- Over £1000 balance: 5.8% net of tax (7.75% gross)
- Between £500 and £999 balance: 4.3% net of tax (5.75% gross)
- Between £100 and £499 balance: 3.2% net of tax (4.25% gross)

No interest is paid on ordinary current accounts by any of the major banks.

Savings accounts

There are various permutations of the ordinary deposit account, each of which is really a marketing exercise to encourage specific categories of people to save with the bank – for example, there are schemes to encourage parents to save for their children, schoolchildren to save for themselves, and engaged couples and newly-weds to save for the deposit on a house. Interest rates are normally similar to seven-day deposit accounts – that is, 5.8% net of tax (7.75% gross).

It is very important to remember that, on all these accounts, bank interest is paid net of tax, *and the tax cannot be reclaimed*. This being the case, except for pure convenience, do not leave your money in a bank if your income is sufficiently low as to attract no tax. It should also be noted that, if you pay tax at the top rate, any bank interest received will be subject to further tax, in addition to that deducted at source.

If you study bank literature, you will find that all the banks offer a number of ancillary services, apart from the direct handling of your money. They have specific departments to give investment advice, set up trust funds, handle share portfolios, make wills and provide insurance. On balance, however, we are not in favour of banks being used for these sorts of facilities. If you want insurance advice, we would recommend that you go direct to an insurance broker. If you want to invest in the Stock Exchange, then acquire a stockbroker. At the risk of appalling generalization, it is our opinion that bank facilities are often not as competitive as they could be, and the advice offered tends to be rather narrow in view. Certainly, one thing you should never expect is investment advice from your local bank manager. If you feel you want to take advantage of such bank facilities, then you must talk direct to their specialist departments.

The main object of this book is to ensure that you can manage your money yourself to the best possible advantage. We would like to feel that, having read it, you have a very clear idea of what you want in terms of investment – at which time, it is simply a question of going shopping for the best possible deal.

6 The building societies

Like the High Street banks, building societies are not the place for high-rate tax payers to put their money. Interest is paid net of tax at the standard rate, but will be grossed up and subject to higher rates, where applicable. Neither should pensioners and others on low incomes and paying no tax put their nest eggs into building societies. For them, the same situation applies as with the banks – they will not be able to recover the tax already deducted.

However, for a vast range of people with a few hundred or a few thousand pounds to invest, the building societies provide a rewarding and convenient place for investment. Regular saving is easy, and of course there is the enormous attraction of preferential treatment when it comes to mortgage facilities if you have saved for your house deposit through a building society. For young people, anticipating the requirement to buy their own home one day, the building society is rightly a very good place to invest in.

Generally, building society accounts, both for investment and saving, are more attractive than bank deposit accounts. Interest rates tend to be higher, and these days, the societies – especially the larger ones – are becoming progressively more competitive with the banks with regard to the services they are offering. Most large building societies now offer cheque and cashing facilities, and will operate standing order payments for you on a monthly basis. In terms of security, the risk of a building society failure is negligible. The larger societies maintain huge reserves and liquid funds to meet contingencies, and are granted trustee status by the Chief Registrar of Building Societies as evidence of their stability; it is worth checking out this trustee status if you are dealing with one of the less well-known societies. However, so far as selecting the right society is concerned, there is little or nothing to choose between them, and frankly, if you are looking at the major societies, the only real criterion to consider is selecting the one that is in the most convenient location.

Money placed in a building society can be put either in a deposit account or in a share account. There are varying kinds of deposit accounts available, and many forms of share accounts, but however described, societies basically offer similar packages. Deposit accounts have the advantage of having the first claim against the assets of the society in case of failure, but consequently earn slightly lower interest than the various sorts of share accounts. As with banks, building societies offer a whole range of interest rates and incentives, but the governing factors remain the same: the more money you have in your account, the longer you are prepared to leave it there and the longer the notice of withdrawal that you are prepared to give, the larger will be your rate of return. Most societies are prepared to be quite flexible on withdrawal, provided the minimum balances are maintained.

Below, we describe the typical range of accounts being operated by the major societies, against which we have quoted rates of interest. *As with the banks, we must stress again that these rates are those that were available at the time of writing this book, when the bank base rate was 11.5 per cent.* The rates quoted here are simply to provide you with a comparison, against which you can judge other forms of investment. When you read this book, interest rates may well have varied considerably in response to market factors, so please do check the up-to-date figures as and when you are ready to invest.

High-yielding share accounts

These accounts offer the highest rates of interest, and you are able to withdraw money on demand. The rate of interest will be governed by the balance maintained, and normally interest is paid annually.

- Over £10,000: 8.50% net of tax (12.0% gross)
- Over £5000: 8.25% net of tax (11.6% gross)
- Over £2000: 8.00% net of tax (11.3% gross)
- Over £500: 7.75% net of tax (10.9% gross)

Subscription share accounts

These accounts are useful for regular monthly saving from a few pounds up to £200–250 per month. The societies encourage people to invest in this form of account by offering a higher rate of interest than that for the ordinary share account (*see below*) because it represents a regular flow of funds, which tend to accumulate rather than being constantly withdrawn. This is an ideal type of account if you are building up savings for a house purchase. Interest, paid annually, is 7% net of tax (9.85% gross).

Ordinary share account

You can open an ordinary share account with virtually any amount of spare cash, and there are no restrictions on withdra-

wals. Interest is usually paid twice yearly at 6% net of tax (8.45% gross).

Operating share account

As already mentioned, most societies these days are offering a range of banking services, such as payment of standing orders, regular savings transfers, the ability to accept credit transfers of monthly salaries, cash-card cashing facilities and normal cheque accounts. Each society describes these current accounts in a different way, but the advantage they have over normal bank current accounts is that they generally pay interest at the same rate as the ordinary share account – the only restriction being the requirement for the maintenance of a minimum balance, usually £100. Of course, the services they offer are not as wide as those of the banks, but if your transactions are simple, there is a lot to be said for using a building society operating share account in preference to a bank current account, for the simple reason that your money is actually working for you. Interest is paid twice yearly at 4.5% net of tax (6.34% gross) for balances up to £2500. Over that figure, net interest is about the same as for the high-yielding share accounts.

Ordinary deposit account

This account has the same degree of flexibility as offered by the ordinary share account but, technically, provides greater security since, in the event of failure, a society has to repay its depositors before settling its share accounts. Frankly, we consider this rather academic, provided you are investing with a well-established building society, and since the interest rate offered is lower, we see no grounds for recommending it. Interest is paid twice yearly at 5.75% net of tax (8.21% gross).

Save-as-you-earn schemes

One or two societies are currently offering 'save-as-you-earn schemes', which are specifically attractive to high-rate tax payers, and which may catch on and be offered by other societies. You contribute a fixed amount each month to the scheme. No interest is paid on the account, but at the end of five years, an untaxed bonus is added to the amount saved. The bonus is equal to fourteen months of your contributions, which is equivalent to net interest of 8.3% per annum (11.69% gross). Unfortunately, the maximum monthly deposit is £20, so the potential tax saving may not be sufficiently large to attract a person with a very high income.

For all the reasons we have stated, building societies do represent a very attractive and secure means of investment and saving, with the added bonus that investing with them does make first-time house purchase easier. However, you should not be too brainwashed by this fact, and if a more attractive investment proposition comes your way, you should not be afraid to take it. During the writing of this chapter, we compared notes with each other and discovered that we had both bought our first homes with the assistance of building society mortgages – without having saved a penny with the societies in question! Certainly, putting your money somewhere other than with a building society does not preclude you from purchasing your own home with building society money as and when you are ready to do so.

7   National Savings

The various National Savings schemes all operate under the umbrella of the Department of National Savings, which, as the name suggests, is government-sponsored and government-backed – it is really a sort of extension of the Treasury. National Savings represent part of the armoury used by governments for raising money. You, the investor, are quite literally encouraged to invest in your country, in return for which the government will pay you for the privilege of borrowing your money.

Virtually all aspects of National Savings are dealt with on a day-to-day basis via the Post Office, and undoubtedly this has been a major factor in encouraging the savings habit nationwide. Most of us, at some stage in our lives, have saved with the Post Office Savings Bank, which has now been re-named the National Savings Bank.

There are several distinct sections within the National Savings movement:

- *The National Savings Bank*
This is based in Glasgow and operates the ordinary accounts, regular customer accounts, investment accounts and deposit bonds.
- *The Savings Certificate Office*
This is in Durham and is responsible for the issue of savings certificates, index-linked savings certificates and yearly plan certificates.
- *The Bonds and Stock Office*
Based in Blackpool, this is responsible for the issue of indexed-income bonds and for the handling of government stocks – 'gilts' (*see* Chapter 8) – on the National Savings Stock Register.

- *The Bonds and Stock Office*

This section, located in Lytham St Annes, deals exclusively with premium bonds, and that most fickle of all characters – ERNIE!

Having identified who deals with what, let us look in detail at the various different types of National Savings available. *Do remember that, as in previous chapters, interest rates are quoted against a bank base rate of 11.5 per cent to give you a means of comparison with other types of investment.* You should check the up-to-date interest position before making any investment commitments.

National Savings Bank ordinary account

The ordinary account is the successor to the old Post Office Savings Bank account. You can open an account at any Post Office by depositing a minimum of £1 and you can keep up to £10,000 in your account. You can withdraw up to £100 in cash, on demand, at any Post Office; larger withdrawals are handled direct by the National Savings Bank in Glasgow, which will send you a warrant that you can pay into a bank or cash at a Post Office.

When you open an ordinary account, you receive a bank book, into which all your deposits and withdrawals are entered. From time to time, the bank book is retained for checking, and this is always the case when you withdraw more than £50 in cash. Interest is calculated on the balance in your account for each complete month. It is credited to the account annually, on 31 December, and will be entered in your bank book when it is next kept for checking. Interest of up to £70 a year, payable to you and to your spouse, is completely tax free, whatever your circumstances. The normal rate of interest is 3 per cent, but a higher rate of 6 per cent is paid in any month you have maintained a balance of at least £500 and provided that you have maintained a minimum balance of at least £100 for the whole year.

National Savings Bank regular customer account

Once you have used your ordinary account at a chosen Post Office for at least six months, you can apply for a regular customer account. This will enable you to draw up to £250 in cash, on demand, at your Post Office, in addition to the normal cashing facilities at other Post Offices. The £250 can be also drawn in Thomas Cook traveller's cheques.

Both ordinary and regular customer accounts do have other benefits. You can organize the payment of standing orders, free of charge, and there is also a 'pay bill service' by which you can pay your bills at the Post Office direct from your account, without actually having to handle any cash.

Certainly the Post Office savings book has become a national institution, and for children and young people particularly, opening an account is the best possible way of demonstrating to them how saving their money will make it grow.

National Savings Bank investment account

If you can manage without the need for instant access to cash from your account, a National Savings investment account is a much more attractive proposition, so far as interest rates are concerned. One month's notice of withdrawal is required, and withdrawal can be made either by crossed warrant or in cash, from a named Post Office. In order to open an investment account, you need a minimum deposit of £5, and the maximum you can keep on the account is £50,000, although this figure may be exceeded by interest credited.

Interest is calculated on a daily basis, and is credited gross on 31 December, the rate currently being 11.5 per cent. All interest is taxable, but the tax is not deducted at source, so in this respect, the National Savings investment account is more attractive for the non-tax payer than a bank or building society deposit or investment account.

National Savings deposit bonds

Deposit bonds are for people wishing to invest lump sums for a minimum of a year, at a premium rate of interest. In order to buy deposit bonds, you must make a minimum purchase of £100, and this applies *every time* you buy a deposit bond. Larger purchases can be made in multiples of £50, up to a maximum of

£50,000 – although this figure may be exceeded by the interest credited.

The main feature of deposit bonds is that you are expected to leave your money with National Savings for at least a year. Once a full year has elapsed, you do not lose any interest when withdrawals are made, but if you withdraw all or part of your bond purchase within a year, you will only earn interest at half the published rate on the amount repaid. The minimum amount that can be withdrawn is £50 and you must give three months' notice in writing of any withdrawal.

In return for this commitment, deposit bonds pay 12 per cent a year, which is calculated on a daily basis and is added to your investment on the anniversary of your bond purchase.

As with the investment account, tax is not deducted at source, so this does make deposit bonds very attractive to the non-tax payer.

National Savings certificates

At the time of writing, National Savings certificates are in their 31st issue. This simply means that every time National Savings certificate rates of interest change, or any of their other terms are revised, a new issue is made, so the figures referred to here will not apply unless you are reading this book while the 31st issue is still available.

The major attraction of National Savings certificates is that they are tax free – both from income tax and capital gains tax. Each certificate costs £25 and the interest rate averages 7.85 per cent if the certificate is kept for five years. Certainly you should aim to keep your certificates for this length of time since this will undoubtedly show the most effective growth rate – as demonstrated in the following table:

Years after purchase	Value of one certificate at end of year	Yield for year (tax free)
1	£26.44	5.76%
2	£28.20	6.66%
3	£30.40	7.80%
4	£33.12	8.95%
5	£36.48	10.14%

It is prohibitive to withdraw your money during the first year, since only the purchase price will be returned and you will gain no interest at all.

You may hold up to £5000 of 31st-issue certificates, though, of course, this may vary with future issues.

One final note on National Savings certificates: if you currently hold any of the 1st–6th issues – on sale between 1916 to 1939 – you should cash them in immediately. They are currently only earning between 1.25 and 2 per cent a year!

National Savings indexed-linked savings certificates

At the time of writing, index-linked savings certificates are in their 3rd issue, and it is on this basis that we have quoted figures. While inflation is well under control, these certificates are probably not very attractive. They claim to be inflation-proof – in other words, as well as receiving a rate of interest, averaging 3.45 per cent compound over five years, you will also receive guaranteed extra interest, index-linked in line with rising prices. You can cash in your savings certificates at any time, but you will receive no interest if withdrawal is made within the first year. Certainly you are encouraged to keep certificates for five years, and the basic rates of interest payable on a year-by-year basis are:

Year 1	2.50%
Year 2	2.75%
Year 3	3.25%
Year 4	4.00%
Year 5	5.25%

You can buy index-linked share certificates for an investment of £25, up to £5000, but you must make your purchases in multiples of £25. Again, the interest on these certificates is tax free.

National Savings yearly plan certificates

These have replaced the old National Savings SAYE scheme, and they do represent quite good tax-free saving.

How do they work? You undertake to invest between £20 and £200 a month by standing order for twelve months, and you will be issued with a yearly plan certificate. If you hold your certificate for a further four years, you will receive the maximum rate of interest. Rates are:

Year 1	6.0%
Year 2	8.5%
Year 3	8.5%
Year 4	8.5%
Year 5	8.5%

The five-year return averages 8.19 per cent, free of tax. Again, if you stop the monthly payments and ask for a withdrawal during the first year, you will receive no interest. After the first year, interest will be calculated up to the point of withdrawal.

National Savings indexed-income bonds

Like the index-linked savings certificates, these are aimed at providing you with an inflation-proof scheme, although it does not appear particularly attractive at the present time. You can invest anything from £5000 to a maximum of £50,000 in multiples of £1000, and on the 20th day of each month you will receive a monthly interest payment. For the first year, the interest, which is paid gross, will be at 8 per cent, and thereafter it will be adjusted to keep pace with inflation. For example, if there was a 5 per cent inflation rate in the first year, a person starting with an income from his/her bonds of £100 a month would receive £105 a month in the second year. At the end of the second year, the £105 would be increased again by a percentage that matched inflation and so on. There is a limit of ten years during which you can hold bonds.

The point we would make here is that, while your income is index-linked, your capital is not: £20,000 invested in this way for ten years would be worth, in a capital sense, comparatively little by the time you finally withdrew it. If you had invested the £20,000 in a cottage in the country, your capital position might be very different indeed. We should point out that, although the interest is paid gross, it *is* subject to tax.

Premium bonds

What can we say? Each bond costs £1, the minimum purchase is £10, and you can hold up to £10,000 worth of bonds. No interest payments are made, but every month someone, somewhere, wins £250,000, and every week a first prize of £100,000, a second prize of £50,000 and a third prize of £25,000 are awarded. There are also smaller prizes of £10,000, £5000, £1000 – down to £50. Heavens above, it has to be worthwhile having a few premium bonds – if for no other reason than to help you daydream your way through a particularly unpleasant, wet Monday!

Children under sixteen cannot buy bonds, but they can have bonds bought for them by parents, legally appointed guardians or grandparents. You can cash in your bonds at any time, but our advice would be that, once you have bought them, file them away and keep your fingers crossed!

So what is our general view of National Savings? It is a good form of investment, particularly for the small saver. Many of the schemes, as we have demonstrated, provide entirely tax-free growth for your savings, and the fact that tax, where applicable, is not deducted at source is an added bonus.

Whether you should make an investment in National Savings depends very largely, we feel, on temperament. Undoubtedly, for best results, you must commit your money on a long-term basis, and this, of course, may not suit those of you with a more volatile lifestyle – you cannot win by chopping and changing with National Savings. Against that, those of us who recognize that long-term investment goes against our own personalities might well benefit from, say, the yearly plan. Having made the commitment to pay so much a month, it forces the issue, and very soon you would reach a point where you simply had to go with it, to maximize the benefit.

Some people worry that National Savings may be affected by changes in government. This is not the case. All governments recognize its importance and, in any case, are knee-deep in legislation designed to ensure that promises made by the National Savings Bank cannot be broken. At the risk of making a political statement, we would say that while, at the moment, the index-linked schemes are not very attractive, with inflation currently running down towards 3 per cent, a change of government could turn the economy upside down and, in an effort to alleviate unemployment, send inflation sky high again. Suddenly the index-linked schemes could become very attractive.

So the message with National Savings is not to commit more money to these schemes than you can genuinely afford. If you are forced to withdraw any sums before the allotted time, it makes a mockery of the whole exercise and you would have been far better investing your money in some short-term, safe home.

8   Gilt-edged securities

The nickname for gilt-edged securities is 'gilts'. What are they? Well, strictly speaking, gilts refer to government stock. There is constant pressure on the government to raise money, and it does this by seeking loans to finance the national debt, the purchase of British Leyland or whatever. It therefore looks to the nation to lend it money, in return for guaranteed interest payments at a fixed rate. However, the word *gilts* now tends to have a slightly more general definition, in that it also includes local authority stocks, Commonwealth government stocks and stocks of public boards such as British Gas, the water authorities and so on. The vast majority of gilts are owned, and dealt in, by the major financial institutions such as banks, insurance companies and pension funds. It is a very professional marketplace, and in our view not really suitable for the amateur or small investor. However, because government stock can be purchased via the Post Office, it has become reasonably popular with small investors, so we intend here to set out for you the pros and cons, to enable you to make your own decision as to its worth as an investment for you.

There is a wide variety of government stock in issue, and each time there is a new issue, it has to be on terms that will make it attractive for financial institutions to buy. Stock is quoted in nominal amounts of £100. During the lifetime of a stock, it will be bought and sold at a variety of prices, which can vary from stock to stock, some rising as high as £140, others dropping to £30. The reason the price varies is because stocks are nearly always issued at fixed rates of interest – referred to as the 'coupon rate' – and the rates of interest can vary from 2½ to

15½ per cent. Clearly the interest rate that is set fluctuates in its attractions according to how the rest of the money market is looking. The other factor that governs the price at which stock can be bought is the redemption date – in other words, the date at which the government will repay the loan. When the government issues stock, not only does it declare the interest rate that will be paid, it also specifies the date on which the loan will be repaid. Since, with few exceptions, the loan is repaid at its nominal value, this obviously affects the stock's worth, particularly as the redemption date approaches.

Gilts are classified under five broad headings:

- *Shorts*: with lives to redemption of up to five years.
- *Mediums*: with lives to redemption of between five and fifteen years.
- *Longs*: with lives to redemption of over fifteen years.
- *Undated*: having no redemption date.
- *Index-linked*: with a small initial coupon (interest rate), which together with the redemption value, is linked to inflation over the life of the stock. Index-linked gilts can be short, medium or long, but are never undated.

The yield on government stock is shown in two ways: the flat yield and the redemption yield. The *flat yield* is the annual interest on the stock, expressed as a percentage of the price of the stock. The *redemption yield* measures not only the interest received but also takes account, on an annual basis, of the profit that will be realized on redemption. The best way to demonstrate these yields is to give you much simplified examples of how they are calculated:

- If 3% Treasury stock with a redemption date of 1990 is priced at £83 three years and nine months before redemption, the *flat yield* is $3\% \times {}^{100}/_{83}$ or 3.61% per annum.
- There would also be a redemption 'profit' of £17 (the difference between £100 and £83), which, spread over the remaining 3¾ years before redemption, would add a further 4.53% to produce a *redemption yield* of 8.14% per annum.

Purchasing this stock for £83 is only worthwhile because it is going to be redeemed in 3¾ years' time, and not because of its 3.61 per cent flat yield, which clearly is not very attractive.

So how do you acquire gilt-edged securities? There are three ways in which you can buy and sell: through a stockbroker; through an agent such as a bank; or through the Post Office, which can buy bonds on your behalf through the National Savings Stock Register. All three will charge you a fee for purchasing stock on your behalf. The Post Office is the cheapest; next come, surprisingly, stockbrokers; and the most expensive of all are the banks.

Clearly, if you do not have a broker, it is most sensible to purchase your stock through the Post Office, particularly when the sum is small. However, unlike at banks and stockbrokers, you cannot purchase more than £10,000 worth of stock through the Post Office in any one day, but there is no limit as to the total amount of stock you may hold. Buying and selling is as easy as filling in a form and handing over your cheque, and once the purchase is completed, you will receive an investment certificate. Yields are quite reasonable compared, for instance, with bank deposit interest and with building society rates. Stocks held on the National Savings Stock Register are easy to buy and sell through the Post Office, and interest on all of the stocks on that register is paid gross (although it is, of course, taxable).

On the face of it, you may consider that gilts represent an attractive investment for the small- or medium-sized investor, and this being the case, you may be wondering at our apparent reluctance to recommend them. This is possibly just because they are complicated. How on earth would Mrs Average know whether to buy 10½% Treasury Stock 1984, 6% Funding Stock 1993 or 3% Redemption Stock 1986–1996? We don't! For the investor with high rates of personal tax, wishing to be free of Capital Gains Tax, and prepared and able to understand the complexities both of the market and his or her own detailed tax position, there are attractions in gilts. However, you do need to have a feel for dealing. You cannot play at it, and as we have said, it is a professional market, largely dominated by the institutions.

Two random points are worth clarifying:

(1) If you happen to find yourself with an old leaflet describing government stock, it may indicate that profits on gilts are sub-

ject to Capital Gains Tax, unless held for more than one year. This is, in fact, no longer the case. They have been free of CGT since 1985.

(2) Although interest on gilts held on the National Savings Stock Register is paid gross, interest on all other stocks is paid net of tax. The exception is 3½% War Loan, for which interest is paid gross. Incidentally, there is no redemption date on War Loan; its current price is around £40, which therefore shows a flat yield of 8.8 per cent.

9 Stocks and shares

Before looking at the various types of stocks and shares available, it probably would be helpful to describe precisely what is meant by the two terms, and how they differ.

Stocks 'Stock' is a rather old-fashioned word. It is normally taken to represent a unit of £100 of debenture or loan, in a company or corporation. Gilts (which we dealt with in the previous chapter) and stocks are very similar, except that the loan is being made to a company rather than to the government. In other words, companies use a very similar device to attract the general public into lending them money.

Shares To own a share is to own a piece of the company whose shares you have bought. Each share in issue is an equal portion of the capital that constitutes the ownership of the company.

On the face of it, shares would seem a safer investment than stocks, but this is not actually so. Most stocks are supported by assets – in other words, either specific assets or the general assets of the company have been secured to repay loans should things go wrong. In the case of shares, if the company in which you have invested goes into liquidation, you are left with your percentage of nothing.

There are three types of *stock*:

(1) *Mortgage or debenture stock*: This is safe, protected stock in that assets are normally pledged against the borrowing, usually in the form of property.

(2) *Unsecured loan stock*: This, as the name suggests, is stock that has been issued without being secured against the assets of the company.

(3) *Convertible loan stock*: This is stock that entitles you, at some future date, to convert your holding into ordinary shares.

There are two principal types of *shares*:

(1) *Ordinary shares*: This is the main block of shares that constitute the ownership of the company, and which are thus termed the equity.

(2) *Preference shares*: Preference shares have no voting rights attached to them, but in the event of a repayment of capital, they rank ahead of ordinary shares. Preference shares are usually entitled to a fixed rate of dividend only, although it is possible for them to be issued in a form that gives them the same dividend entitlement as ordinary shares.

Investment in stocks and shares falls naturally into two distinct sections – those investments that are made in companies listed on the Stock Exchange, and those investments made in companies that are not listed.

Investing in companies listed on the Stock Exchange

Before looking in detail at the types of investment you can make in listed companies, let us first consider the implications of a Stock Exchange investment. There is a tendency for us to think in rather glamorous terms about the Stock Exchange – as the place where fortunes are made and lost, a world apart, a centre for wheeling and dealing. This is not strictly true – try and think of it more in terms of a street market. Its function is simple: to provide the means by which the savings of the public can be made available to companies that need finance. It is also not nearly as volatile as one is often led to believe; in fact, it is the long-term investment on the Stock Exchange that is most likely to be really effective, not the purported frantic buying and selling.

So what advantages do you stand to gain from investment in equities generally, and in the stock market in particular? The main benefit is that your investment will act as a hedge against

inflation. If you invest your money in a bank or a building society, it will almost certainly produce you a far better immediate return than you will receive from the buying of shares. However, the pound you place in your bank today will still only be a pound in five years' or ten years' time. In other words, the amount of your capital remains unchanged, whatever happens to inflation. However, if your money is invested in a successful company, your capital will keep pace with inflation and, indeed, may be even outstrip it. Let's look now at the various types of investment in companies listed on the Stock Exchange.

Ordinary shares (equities)

Buying ordinary shares in a listed company is likely to give you a yield of about 3½–4 per cent per annum. Compared with the kind of interest you will receive by investing your money elsewhere, this may not seem very high, but as already mentioned, your capital will grow as well. It is important to understand the difference between buying an ordinary share and investing in, say, a building society. When you buy a share, it is not because you are looking for a fixed rate of interest in return for the loan of your money. You buy a share in a company because you believe in its future ability to produce

69

profits, and your share entitles you, quite literally, to *share* in those profits and in the growth of the company. When shares are issued on to the Stock Exchange for the first time, they are given a *face value* which could be 25p, £1, £5 or whatever. As the shares are subsequently bought and sold, they assume their own fluctuating value: if the company is doing well, the shares rise; if it is doing badly, they fall.

At whatever price you purchase your shares, when the company announces a distribution of profit, it expresses that distribution as a percentage of the original face value, or sometimes simply in pence per share. Distribution of profits is made twice a year in the form of *dividends*. As the dividend payment rises, so should the value (current price) of the shares, though it needs to be borne in mind that the company will only ever distribute *some* of its profits to shareholders, varying proportions being kept on one side for the future expansion of the company. What a company has to do is to pay sufficient dividends to make the shares attractive and therefore encourage investment in the company, without in any way undermining the capital structure of the company.

So what is the minimum amount of money you can sensibly invest on the Stock Exchange? There are two ways of looking at it. If you have a lump sum to invest, then, frankly, we would not recommend your considering the Stock Exchange unless you have more than £10,000 available. However, there is room for the smaller investor if you can invest a reasonable sum annually. For example, if you have £2000 to £3000 surplus cash available from your income each year, then steady, careful investment on an annual basis is a very worthwhile exercise – which brings us to the scheme recently introduced: the Personal Equity Plan.

Personal Equity Plan (PEP)

The 1986 Budget introduced the Personal Equity Plan as a means of encouraging wider share ownership and an increased general level of investment on the Stock Exchange. From January 1987, you can invest up to £2400 a year in buying ordinary shares quoted on any UK Stock Exchange, or on the

Unlisted Securities Market (*see* p. 73). Provided you hold the shares for at least one full calendar year and reinvest all dividends and all the proceeds from any disposal, your income and profits will be completely tax free. It remains to be seen whether the cost of operating a PEP will be justified by the savings in income tax and Capital Gains Tax, but our view is that this will prove to be a very effective way for many individuals to make their first sortie into stock market trading. We would, however, strongly recommend that, bearing in mind the limited size of PEP, you should stay with quoted shares and keep away from the Unlisted Securities Market.

New issues

It is always worthwhile looking at the new issues of ordinary shares – that is, shares being offered on the Stock Exchange for the first time – when a company first 'goes public'. The most spectacular of these in recent years was the British Telecom flotation, where people were scrabbling for their share of the new issue. New issues are usually a sound investment, because the company in question is anxious to make the issue price of the shares look as attractive as possible in order to encourage investors. Once acquired, the shares are almost certain to increase in value, at any rate initially. Of course you cannot build up a portfolio based entirely on new issues since you have no control over the timing of your investment, nor will you have much idea of the amount of your allocation, but it is worthwhile keeping a look out for them.

Options

Instead of buying and selling shares, it is possible to deal in options on shares – in other words, you pay for the right to purchase shares at some definite future date at an agreed price. If the shares go up beyond the agreed price, you can exercise your option to buy at your lower price, and then sell immediately at a profit if you so wish. If the shares fail to reach the agreed price, you can cut your losses – which will only mean the loss of your option payment. If the shares rise beyond the agreed price during the option period, the option itself clearly has a value, and you can actually sell the option to make a profit. Frankly, this is not a market for the average individual investor, but it is important that you know what is meant by the term.

Fixed-interest securities

Fixed-interest securities refer to company debentures, unsecured loan stocks, convertible loan stocks and preference shares – in other words, we are not looking here at ordinary shares but at stock and preference shares. In our view, there is no real attraction here for the small-to-medium investor. The yield is normally higher than ordinary shares, but this is partly because there is no potential for capital growth and partly because there is very little dealing in these securities – which means you will be buying into something for which there is very little demand. If a particular stock is actively traded, then the yield will drop. In our view, you would be far better advised to put your money into equally attractive, and far easier, fixed-interest investments, such as the building society and National Savings schemes.

So these, then, represent the main areas of stock market investment, and now is the time for us to jump down off the fence and try and give you some general advice on stock market investment. We have already lectured you on the fact that the Stock Exchange is no place to get rich quick. One problem is that you can buy shares in a good company at the right price, but that price can go up or down merely in response to the trend of the market, irrespective of the performance of the company itself. You can make a lot of money, but you can lose it, too, and we would strongly recommend that you never invest more in the stock market than you can actually afford to lose. At best, it is fun. There is enormous satisfaction in opening the newspaper to see how your investment is doing, and of course, you can invest in companies that reflect your own personal taste. If you have a specialist knowledge of any particular industry or a liking for a particular country, these preferences can be reflected in your share portfolio.

If you genuinely have several thousand pounds available for investment on a regular basis each year, it is very tempting now to suggest you should 'have a go', particularly with the introduction of PEP. Do not be tempted to invest a lesser sum, though – you do need to spread your risk over several shares, and the costs involved in a series of small purchases would make the possible profits unattractive.

A glossary of the terms connected with Stock Exchange dealing, which we hope you will find helpful, can be found in the Appendix, and we will be discussing the role of stockbrokers in detail on pp. 103–6.

Investing in companies not listed on the Stock Exchange

The Unlisted Securities Market (USM)

Before a company can be listed on the Stock Exchange, it is subjected to a very thorough examination to ensure the stability of its financial position. The USM is a marketplace dealing in shares of companies that, for various reasons, do not qualify for listing under the very strict requirements of the Stock Exchange. They may be too small or too young, and while they are certainly not 'fly by night' affairs, they do carry a somewhat second-class label. Frankly, we would not recommend that you invest in USM shares unless you have some specialist inside knowledge of the company concerned. Buying shares is a risky enough business – there is no need to multiply the risk factor.

Business Expansion Scheme

This is an extremely tax-effective scheme for those with very high incomes, and has been introduced in order to help small businesses raise risk capital. Individuals paying UK income tax can receive tax relief by subscribing for new ordinary shares in companies with which they have no close connections. They can invest up to £40,000 in any one year, and can claim the sum as a reduction of their taxable income. The minimum amount of money that you can put into any company is £500, and shares must be retained for at least five years in order to receive full tax relief. If they are sold too soon, relief may be withdrawn or reduced.

Not all companies are eligible for the Business Expansion Scheme. It is necessary for them to be incorporated in the UK and to be resident in the UK only. Their shares may not be quoted on the Stock Exchange or traded on the Unlisted Securities Market. A company must carry on its trade only, or mainly, in the UK, and certain types of trade are exempt, such as banking, leasing, hiring, property dealing and development, insurance, accountancy and legal services, together with farming trades.

There are two ways in which you can become involved in the Business Expansion Scheme. Either you can deal direct with an individual company – which, assuming the company succeeds, is likely to prove the most lucrative method – or you can join one of the many newly formed BES funds. A number of stockbrokers, merchant banks and insurance companies have jumped on the bandwagon of the Business Expansion Scheme by forming and managing portfolios of investments in private companies. This means you are investing, not in one company, but in several. Normally the minimum subscription is £2000, and although the investment is likely to be less exciting than dealing directly with one company, at least the risk is being spread over a number of different businesses.

What advice can we give on the Business Expansion Scheme? One of the most important areas to consider is how easy it will be to dispose of your shares at the end of five years – assuming this is what you wish to do. There is a very limited market for private company shares; buying in is one thing, but you need to feel you can get out as and when you need to. Again, there is the question of temperament to consider. Although the Business Expansion Scheme has been very successful in generating capital for private companies, it is a very risky business. We would go so far as to recommend that, if you have no commercial experience (if, to put it bluntly, you cannot read a balance sheet), you should not be looking at this form of investment. It does require a degree of commercial cunning. If you are making a direct investment in a company, make sure that the Inland Revenue has issued a certificate confirming that it is a qualifying company under BES rules.

Investment in private companies

This may not sound very patriotic, at a time when we are all being encouraged to support entrepreneurs, but we strongly recommend that you do not become involved in a minority interest in a private company. As already mentioned in the section on the Business Expansion Scheme, there is very little market for shares in private companies. It is easy enough to buy them, but very difficult to sell them. You can all too easily find yourself locked in with no dividend payment – indeed, no financial benefit at all – and no hope of that position altering. If you must become involved in a private company, then you should insist on having a minimum of 25 per cent of the equity. Shareholders owning this percentage can convene shareholders' meetings and they can ultimately block decisions on such issues as capital reconstruction. While all shareholders have legal rights, it is only if you have 25 per cent or more of the equity that you really have any opportunity to exercise them. Ideally, of course, you should have a 51 per cent shareholding, in which case you can control the company, but as a private investor, this is unlikely. Be warned, and avoid this area like the plague, and especially avoid investing in friends' businesses. It colours your judgement and all too often ends in disaster.

Employee share schemes

This is where employees are offered shares, and options, in the company that employs them. There are a variety of circumstances – some of which are very tax-effective – in which an employee may be granted shares, and almost without exception, terms tend to be extremely favourable.

We are very much in favour of employee participation. If you are offered shares by your employer, we would strongly recommend that you seriously consider the offer. However, if you build up a valuable holding in company shares, do be very clear on the tax implications, and take advice, before selling them.

75

Of all the varying types of investments, stocks and shares are, with doubt, the most exciting, particularly if you have a genuine interest in commerce. This is really the crux of the matter: you really do need to be business-orientated to invest on the stock market. This does not mean that you have to be involved in some high-powered job yourself, but you should be genuinely interested in the way companies operate, how they make their profits and how their fortunes ebb and flow. If this whole area is a mystery to you and, in fact, interests you not at all, then money in stocks and shares is going to be nothing but a worry. You would be far better looking at some form of investment that you understand and upon which you can rely.

10   Unit trusts

A unit trust is a very simple way of investing in stocks and shares. It also enables small investors to put their money into a wide range of stocks and shares, thus spreading both the risks and the opportunities. Individuals can invest relatively small sums, which together form the unit trust fund and which are then invested in bulk by professional managers. Not only is the fund expertly managed, it is also secure, safeguarded by trustees and operated under regulations imposed by the Department of Trade and Industry.

A unit trust fund is open-ended: if you decide to invest £500, your money, together with all the other applications for that day, will swell the fund. If, like you, everyone is buying and few people are selling, the fund will expand, new units will be created to match the inflow of finance and more cash will be available to purchase additional underlying investments. The reverse happens if everyone is in a selling mood.

The price of the units is a direct reflection of the value of the assets on a daily basis. In simple terms, the calculation is made by taking the market value of each investment and dividing the total by the number of units that are currently in issue.

Looking through the range of unit trusts available, it would appear that £500 is the minimum you can invest initially in a unit trust, but once your balance is over this figure, you can add to it via a monthly saving plan by as little as £20 a month. You can buy into unit trusts by making a direct application to the managers or through your bank or a stockbroker, and you can sell in the same way, at any time.

THE SIZE OF THE BATCH MAY VARY, BUT NOT THE INGREDIENTS.

Dividends are normally paid twice a year, after deduction of income tax, at the basic rate, but here is an important point for the non-tax payer – it is possible to claim back this tax from the Inland Revenue. This contrasts with the composite interest paid by the banks and building societies, on which no tax can be reclaimed. While your money is invested in units, you will not be liable for any Capital Gains Tax, however much profit you are making. However, once you sell the units, you will be liable to CGT, if the gain you have made exceeds the CGT exemption limit.

As with stocks and shares, you can expect no more from a unit trust invested in a wide range of general equities than a 3.5–4 per cent yield. For small transactions, especially regular savings, the costs of buying and selling are far less than if you were dealing direct with the Stock Exchange. Unit trust managers usually make an initial charge of about 5 per cent on a purchase, plus a small annual percentage charge against the trust's total income, details of which will be shown in their reports to you.

There are now over 600 different unit trusts, and although they all offer the small investor the benefits of a spread of investment in stocks and shares, do bear in mind the degree to which many unit trust funds specialize in certain types of investment. While this specialization might suit you, it equally might not. It is therefore very important that you pick and choose your unit trust to suit your own particular needs. There are trust funds that quite specifically offer a wide range of investments, others that specialize in a high-income return, others that may concentrate investments in a particular part of the world, or in certain types of industry. A good unit trust should state its investment objective very precisely, and show you a performance record. Do bear in mind that, while on the face of it, a high-income unit trust would appear very attractive, high income is always paid at the expense of capital growth – in other words, your money will be mostly invested in preference shares. This may be exactly the kind of investment for which you are looking, but do not be hoodwinked into assuming that a high-income trust fund is more successful than the rest. A recent report on unit trust performance during 1985 showed that the average trust rose by 8 per cent, but far more revealing was the difference in performance of the various unit trusts: in the same period, the best trust rose by 70 per cent and the worst fell by 45 per cent. This demonstrates a considerable variation in performance, and stresses the need for you to choose wisely.

So, do we recommend unit trusts? For the small investor – and by small, we mean £10,000 or less – yes. Unit trusts are quoted in the national newspapers, so you can follow the development of your investment. The fact that you have no control over how your money is invested can, in itself, be quite attractive, since it reduces the hassle and worry of making those sorts of decisions for yourself. It is, if you like, a halfway house – giving you the feel of investing in stocks and shares, but with the very minimum of risk. Traditionally, unit trusts do not fail, and while their yield may vary, you can be reasonably confident of the average return we have quoted you, provided you choose an established general fund. It is not an exciting investment, but it is safe, and the fact that your capital is protected is of considerable value.

11   Investment trusts

The function of investment trusts is very similar to unit trusts, in as much that they allow the individual investor to place his or her money into a portfolio of shares that is handled by investment managers, thus obtaining the same attractive spread of investments offered by unit trusts.

Unlike unit trusts, however, investment trusts are companies, and when you place your money with them, you actually buy a piece of the company. As our illustration demonstrates, you acquire a piece of the cake, rather than buying individual scones.

As we explained, unit trusts only rise and fall in value as a result of the market price of the shares they hold at any one time. In the case of investment trusts, however, the value of your shares is governed by the success of the investment company and its rating in the market. In other words, it is like buying a share in any company – whether the company is manufacturing clothes, cars or leather handbags, the value of your share will depend on how good the company is at its job. Investment companies are exactly the same. If they are good at investing your money and make substantial profits, then shares in the company will become more valuable. The exact market value of the company's portfolio, and hence the net asset value of the company, is a measure of its success but does not directly affect the price of its shares.

There are fewer investment trusts than unit trusts – about 200 in all – and for some reason, they are not as fashionable as unit trusts. There is no good reason for this: their returns are largely comparable and they represent no greater risk to the saver. On the whole, they seem to attract the slightly richer investor, though here again there is no particular reason for this.

The sensible minimum investment is £1000, and one or two trusts have monthly saving schemes for as little as £15 a month. As with unit trusts, dividends are paid twice yearly and produce roughly the same yield of about 3.5–4 per cent from a general equity fund. There is quite considerable variation among types of investment trust, however, and it is advisable to pick a well-established company. A report for 1985 showed that the average investment trust rose by 14 per cent over the whole year – the best trust rising by 31 per cent and the worst falling by 33 per cent. So do be sure to pick a company with a good track record.

Buying into investment trusts can be done via your bank or a stockbroker, and you can sell at any time. As with unit trusts, your capital is protected, and certainly for long-term investment, it does represent a far more attractive option than keeping your money in a bank or building society. Income tax at the basic rate is deducted at source from your dividends, but you are able to reclaim this if you are a non-tax payer. When you sell your shares you will be liable to Capital Gains Tax if your gains for the year have exceeded the exemption level.

Some investment companies offer what is called a *split-level trust*, or *dual trust*. This means that the investment trust company has two classes of shares: income shares and capital shares. For a fixed period (usually twenty years), those owning the capital shares are entitled to the growth in the assets but have no right to the income. At the end of twenty years, the income shares are paid out at a pre-arranged figure, which is usually at par – in other words, the price you originally paid for them – while the capital shares should have made a substantial gain. Split-level trust shares are quite a good investment. The income shares should produce a growing return, the yield being high enough to act as a good hedge against inflation. The capital shares should result in a good surplus, and are, of course, particularly useful to the high-rate tax payer.

Both unit trusts and investment trusts represent some risk compared with putting your money in a bank. This is not only because there is the slim possibility that you might lose your money if something goes wrong; there is also the fact that nothing is guaranteed. Banks and building societies quote the amount of interest they are going to pay you. This, of course, varies according to the bank base rate, but you always know in advance what you can expect to receive. With unit trusts and investment trusts, there is no guarantee that you will receive anything, nor is there any guarantee that your capital will be protected, and unlike dealing direct with the stock market, you have no control over how your money is used.

Having said that, we are prepared to go out on a limb and say that investment trusts and unit trusts do not go bust – it is their performance levels you need to watch. If you are not sure which trust to put your money with, look for a household name, a big company that you know is well established, and study their track record before committing yourself.

12   Life assurance and bonds

Assurance is the word most relevant here. When you sign up a life assurance policy, you are *assured* of certain things: the insurance company *assures* you that you will receive an *assured* sum of money after a certain number of years, or on your death; you are *reassured* that your family will be protected whatever happens to you. Life assurance is a blend of investment and peace of mind.

There are various types of life assurance. With *whole life assurance*, monthly, quarterly or annual premiums are paid for life, or up to an agreed age, in return for which the sum assured will be payable on death or when the person reaches an agreed age. With a *term life assurance* policy, monthly, quarterly or annual premiums are paid for an agreed term of years – say, five, ten or twenty – and the sum assured will be payable on death during that term in which event, premiums cease.

Endowment policies

There are two types of endowment policies: *fixed* (non-profit) policies and *with-profits* policies. In both cases, monthly, quarterly or annual premiums are paid for a specific number (or term) of years, at the end of which a sum of money is payable. In the event of death during the term, the sum assured is paid and premiums cease.

Fixed endowment policies

A fixed endowment policy is a way of protecting your family in the event of your death and, at the same time, saving for the future. The premiums you pay over the years will provide a guaranteed fixed benefit, which is paid to you on maturity of the policy – say, on retirement. You have the comfort of knowing such a nest egg exists, and that you are covered for life while the policy is running.

With-profits endowment policies

If you have a with-profits endowment policy, you will be paid a bonus, or a series of bonuses, over and above the guaranteed sum assured. These bonuses are based upon the profits of the insurance company, and in practice, a with-profits policy is certainly better value for money than a fixed policy. The premiums paid are absorbed into the general funds of the insurance company, so the level of bonuses declared, both during the term of the policy and at the end of the policy period, will reflect the company's general commercial and investing success. No figures are guaranteed as to bonus payments, so the best way of analysing potential future bonuses is to look at a company's track record over previous years. With-profits policies obviously require higher premiums than fixed policies.

Endowment mortgages

An endowment policy can be used to support a mortgage. With a conventional mortgage from, say, a building society, you pay a monthly sum, which is partly interest on the loan and partly a repayment of the capital sum borrowed. An endowment mortgage works in a different way. Say you borrow £30,000 over twenty years. Each month you will have to pay the interest on £30,000 worth of borrowing, but you make no capital repayments. Instead, you take out an endowment policy for the same sum over the same period, and pay a fixed premium for this. At the end of twenty years, when the endowment policy matures, you use the proceeds to pay off your mortgage in full. If you take out a with-profits endowment policy to support your mortgage, you have the potential advantage of ending up with surplus money when your mortgage is paid off – in other words, your policy premiums will be sufficient to pay off the mortgage, and the bonuses will be surplus. This, of course, is not the case with a fixed policy, but you could take the view that your house will be growing in value in its own right, and therefore you do not need to pay the higher premiums that a with-profits policy will demand.

While we are discussing mortgages, it would also be sensible to remind you of the other elements of insurance – such as accident, disability and permanent health cover – many of which may be covered by a standard home owners' policy. However, while you are considering life assurance, it would be worthwhile checking your general position.

The benefits paid out by a life assurance policy are not subject to Capital Gains Tax, provided the policy meets certain Inland Revenue rules as to the amount and timing of premiums, and the relationship between the premiums and the life cover being offered. Such policies are known as *qualifying life assurance policies* and it is obviously important that you look at this aspect very carefully, especially if, during the same period, you will be disposing of other items that could attract Capital Gains Tax and therefore push you over the exemption figure.

Investment-linked assurance policies

A development of the original with-profits endowment policy is the investment-linked assurance policy, in which, instead of the premiums being absorbed into a general fund, they are allocated to a specific investment fund such as unit trust, so that each premium goes partly to secure the ordinary life cover and partly to buy units in the fund. With an investment-linked policy, the amount payable when the policy matures (or on prior death) will be either the guaranteed sum assured or the value of the underlying units, whichever is the greater.

Life assurance has to be part of every family's thinking. It is, if you like, investment in security, and generally it is very favourably treated by the tax man. It is impossible to try and relate the return you will receive from an endowment policy against, say, the benefits of a unit trust, because so much will depend on your circumstances. The terms will vary enormously, according to your age, your health, whether you are a smoker, the nature of your job and your hobbies. For this reason, you should shop around for the best possible quotation, either by approaching insurance companies direct, or by using an insurance broker (*see* p. 107). We would strongly recommend that you employ the services of the latter, who will cost you no more than dealing direct with an insurance company.

Annuities

Annuities are single-premium non-qualifying life assurance policies. In fact, they are a sort of life assurance in reverse. Instead of paying regular premiums over a number of years, with a view to obtaining a lump sum either on death or at a stated age, the annuitant pays a capital sum to an insurance company in exchange for receiving regular payments for the remainder of his or her life or for a fixed period.

As with life assurance, it is not possible to quote figures because so much depends on the age and circumstances of the annuitant. The most simple forms of annuities provide a high fixed return and, because of inflation, are perhaps mainly suitable for elderly people. Some kinds of annuities can be attractive for younger people in certain circumstances, but we would not recommend them as a general rule (however, *see* 'School fees insurance' *below*). So far as the tax position on annuities is concerned, each payment made to the annuitant will consist of partly capital and partly income – the income element being effectively the interest on the lump-sum premium – and this split is agreed with the tax man so that only the income portion is taxed.

Annuities are often used to unlock capital tied up in a house, when an elderly couple have been retired for some time on a fixed income. While they may hold a very valuable asset in their house, with inflation they face an increasing erosion of day-to-day real income to cope with their expenditure. The response to this problem – which is an increasing one as people live longer – is the creation of the *home income plan*. The annuitant takes out a mortgage with an insurance company and the sum so raised is used to buy an annuity. This means, obviously, that the amount of income the annuitant receives will be reduced by the interest on the mortgage, but none the less, it does produce much needed extra income. Home income plans are restricted by law to people aged sixty-five years and over, although in practice companies do not recommend them until prospective annuitants are in their early seventies.

Investment bonds

An investment bond is also a single-premium non-qualifying life assurance policy. You can buy an investment bond from an insurance company for as little as £500–1000 by a single premium payment. A relatively small part of that payment is utilized to provide life cover – the sum assured only representing the amount you are investing plus a very small excess – say, 10 per cent. The balance of the premium you have paid is invested. The underlying investments can be tangible assets such as property or a range of stocks and shares, unit trusts, or gilts, thus giving a spread of industry, a spread of risk and a spread of income and growth potential. In this respect, the concept of the investment bond is similar to that of the unit trust, in that you place a sum of money in the hands of professional investment managers, and as with unit trusts, there are different types of bonds, some presenting no risk but slow growth, others high risk with large growth potential.

However, having made the decision as to which type of bond you require, you do not need to exercise your judgement as to individual investments – the rest is done for you. The judgement you have to make is whether you are investing with the right company. It is very important when buying an investment bond to make sure that the insurance company you deal with is sound and reputable, because the investments in the bond fund may be simply a part of the general assets of the company. This being the case, if other sections of the company's business are not doing well, then the bond holder could be affected. In reputable companies, the underlying investments supporting the bonds are usually maintained by the insurance company in a separate bond fund, which offers protection for the bond holder and ensures that the performance of the bond fund can be measured independently of other company activities. You should also study very carefully a prospective company's performance record, both in general terms and, in particular, the performance of the bond that interests you.

The tax treatment of investment bonds is somewhat complex and we would suggest that before reading the next few sentences, you wrap a damp towel round your head and concentrate very hard! You can withdraw up to 5 per cent of the original investment each year, free from any tax, and this 5 per cent allowance is cumulative so that you can choose to draw nothing for, say, six years and then draw 30 per cent. You cannot draw more than 100 per cent of the initial investment in this tax free form.

When you cash in the whole of your bond – and incidentally, you can do this at any time, though we would recommend you keep it for at least five years – the overall gain realized (including any amounts already withdrawn) is free of income tax at the standard rate, and free of Capital Gains Tax. However, the gain will be subject to tax at higher rates (40% plus) if you fall into this tax category. Now to the heavy stuff. To calculate how much tax you will have to pay on the gain, you first divide the gain by the number of years the bond has been running; this will give you the 'slice' of gain taxable in the realization year. Then calculate how much tax you would have to pay, with and without that slice in that year, and take one from the other – in other words, establish how much extra tax the slice attracts. From that extra tax, deduct tax on the slice at the basic rate, and this will leave you the amount of tax payable at higher rates. This sum should then be multiplied by the number of years the bond has been running, to arrive at a final amount of tax payable on the whole gain. This whole ghastly process is known as *top slicing*.

Believe it or not, there is still one further point on tax treatment with regard to investment bonds. You will recall that, in Chapter 3, we mentioned that age allowance is reduced when income exceeds a certain level – £9400 in 1986/87. Unfortunately the total taxable gain realized when cashing bonds, without any 'top slicing' calculation being allowed, is regarded as income in the realization year for the purposes of evaluating age allowance. In certain circumstances, therefore, age allowance may be reduced or lost altogether for that year. However, conversely, in earlier years when the 5 per cent tax free withdrawal is made, there is no reduction in age allowance.

Investment bonds do have an attraction, particularly for higher-income earners, but as with most investments, timing is crucial. Where an investment bond can come into its own is, say, with a man in his fifties, whose earnings are high. He could buy into investment bonds, drawing his tax-free 5 per cent as and when appropriate, and then cash the bonds on his retirement; then, his income would drop substantially, and since investment bonds only attract the higher rate of tax, he would not be penalized too heavily at the cashing-up point.

Investment bonds do give quite a high degree of flexibility, and this can be enhanced by buying a number of different bonds which we would recommend you do if you are investing a relatively large sum of money (£10,000 or more). However, do not look on investment bonds as a source of income; their essential function is to provide capital growth.

Friendly society bonds

Friendly societies were originally formed by groups of people wanting to do specific things, their motives being unconnected with profit or personal gain. The Round Table is a sort of friendly society: over the years, their function has changed, but they have still maintained their tax-free status. A small range of bonds is available from friendly societies, on which you pay no tax at all. These bonds are limited in value since they are so tax-effective – indeed, the sum assured must be no more than £750, although a husband and wife are each allowed to take up a bond. The bonds must run for ten years.

There is one particular scheme currently available as a result of a joint venture between a building society and a friendly society. For an annual investment of £200 – i.e. a total of £2000 over ten years – they forecast a tax-free gain after the 10 years of something approaching another £2000. They point out that, if their bond had been available for the ten years up to 1984, it would have produced a net return of over 15 per cent compound per annum – a very sound investment indeed. Another friendly society bond is offering to provide tax-free investment for the benefit of young children. Under the scheme, an investment of £100 a year for ten years is projected to produce over £2000. After ten years, premiums cease and the bond continues to grow, free of tax. It is projected to be worh £8000 after twenty years and is known as a *baby bond*.

School fees insurance

There are a number of specialist schemes available that are designed for those who want to plan some years ahead and make provision for the payment of school fees. The schemes fall into two categories, depending upon whether you wish to set aside income over the next few years so that at least something will be available at the time school fees become payable, or whether you have a capital sum available for immediate investment to create some sort of fund for the future fees. An important point to make is that, for either type of scheme, you do need to be thinking ten years ahead to be really effective in your planning. The time scale can be shortened, but not without losing much of the benefit.

The first type of scheme involves setting aside a fixed amount each year. This is done by taking out a with-profits endowment policy (or policies) that will mature at the time school fees become due. If you have a child of three, for instance, the premiums will be paid by you over the next ten years, and the benefits will be paid *to* you in equal instalments over the following five years. This arrangement could be modified to provide increasing levels of benefit over the five-year period, but that would obviously call for an increase in premium or a restriction in the benefits paid at the start of the five years in order to fund higher benefits in the final years. An alternative means of funding this type of scheme is to arrange a series of separate policies, the first maturing after ten years, the second after eleven years and so on. In that case, premiums would continue to be paid beyond the original ten-year term into the period of schooling, but at a progressively reducing rate.

Meeting school fees by means of endowment policies has no particular tax benefit, but it is an effective, formalized way of saving. It is worth bearing in mind that, if an elderly aunt or grandparent can be persuaded to contribute all or part of the premiums by way of a covenant, a 29 per cent saving can be achieved. A premium of £2000 a year paid by means of a covenant would cost £1420 (£2000 less the standard rate of tax), but the tax of £580 would be recoverable because of the child's personal allowance, thus making the full £2000 available to meet the premium.

The second type of scheme calls for a lump sum to be paid immediately, and is effected through an investment bond. As with the endowment method, a single bond can be purchased to be cashed in over a five-year period. Alternatively, five separate bonds can be taken out, designed to be realized individually over five consecutive years.

You can obtain details of the various schemes we have outlined from your bank, direct from insurance companies or via an insurance broker. Do look at the whole question of life assurance and bond investment in the context of a shopping expedition. There is a considerable variety in the schemes being offered, and it is well worth taking the time to study the various options available before making a firm decision.

13   Your pension

What is a pension? It is a regular income that commences on your retirement, having been provided for by regular contributions during your working life. With the increasing tendency for us to live to a ripe old age, governments are very anxious to avoid our becoming a burden on the state in our dotage. This being the case, they actively encourage pension provision – which means pensions are very tax-effective.

Buying a house is a long-term project, but we have already described it as being a remarkably effective investment – perhaps the best you will ever make. Hard on its heels is your pension fund, *provided you can afford to save money now for your old age*. Compare pension saving with other forms of investment. Suppose you are fifty-three years old and in good health, with quite a comfortable income (paying tax at 50 per cent) and are about to receive a £4500 bonus or profit share. You are thinking of applying this sum to some form of investment – do not look further than your pension scheme.

If you draw your bonus, how much will you actually receive? At your tax level, the net amount of your bonus will suddenly be no more than £2250. So what are your investment alternatives? National Savings certificates because you can expect about 8 per cent per annum, tax free? An investment bond because in twelve years' time you can cash it in when you retire and your income becomes lower? Perhaps – *but the fact remains that you will still only be investing £2250*. If you are salaried, the answer is to ask your company to pay £5000 into their pension scheme for you – that represents the £4500 bonus plus your employer's National Insurance cost. Taking today's figures, we estimate that a £5000 single premium, paid into the pension fund of any of the major life assurance companies, will be worth more than £28,000 by the time you are sixty-five – equivalent to an additional pension of over £4000 a year. Can you match that with your £2250?

We have assumed that you are a relatively high tax payer and a salaried employee, but the attractions are still there if you have a more modest income and pay tax at the standard rate. Equally, if you are self-employed, with earnings to spare, your personal pension plan is just as easy to organize and just as effective. We quoted an example of someone receiving a lump sum bonus, but you do not need a one-off payment of several thousand pounds in order to contribute to a pension scheme. An additional pension contribution of just a few pounds every month into an existing scheme will soon build up substantial funds for you on retirement.

In this particular example, we assumed another thing – that very few people, whether employed or self-employed, have a pension scheme that has already secured the maximum pension allowed by the Inland Revenue. To enable you to work out whether you are allowed to augment your pension arrangements, here are brief details of the main features of the Inland Revenue requirements for company and self-employed pension schemes.

Company pension schemes

- Your pension may be up to the value of two-thirds of final pensionable salary, provided that your total service with the company exceeds ten years.
- You may convert part of that entitlement into a tax-free cash sum, payable on retirement, and equal to 1½ times the final pensionable salary – provided that total service has been at least twenty years.
- In the event of death after retirement, a widow's (or widower's) continuing pension may be two-thirds of the maximum pension that could have been approved for the employee.

- In the event of death while still in employment, a widow's (or widower's) pension may be two-thirds of the maximum pension that would have been payable to the employee if he/she had retired due to ill health at the time of death.
- In addition to the widow's (widower's) pension in either of the above circumstances, a dependant may receive a pension, but this, when added to the widow's pension, may not exceed the amount of the employee's pension.
- In the event of death while still in employment, a lump sum of £5000 or four times the current salary may be paid – whichever is the greater.
- Post-retirement pensions may escalate in line with the cost of living, or at 5 per cent per annum, whichever is the greater.

Your company pension scheme may not provide all of these benefits or, even if it does, you may not have been with the company long enough to have become entitled to full benefit. Alternatively, the scheme might not have been operating long enough to give you full benefit. In any of these events, you are perfectly entitled to make an additional voluntary contribution, or the company may opt to make an additional contribution to improve your benefits – in other words, there are plenty of options available.

Your company scheme may be wholly paid for by the company, or you may also make contributions towards it. However, this is the golden rule: *in order for you to receive tax relief on your contributions (including any additional voluntary payments), your contributions may not exceed 15 per cent of your annual gross earnings*. A word of caution: in comparing your existing pension benefits with the maximum levels allowed by the Inland Revenue, you must take into account the value and effect of any paid-up pension benefits that you may have from previous employments.

A lump sum payment made by the company to augment your pension arrangements (such as the £5000 in our example) does not necessarily have to be put into the company's general fund, nor do any additional voluntary payments that you may make regularly or from time to time. A separate approved scheme can be opened for such purposes. It is very important that you receive from your employers, the company's brokers or the trustees, full details of the additional benefits that will be secured for you by any of these arrangements.

Do insist on a thorough understanding of your company's pension scheme. Particularly if you are some years away from retirement, there is a tendency to be complacent about pension arrangements, not realizing what an enormously effective means of saving and investment they can prove to be.

Self-employed pensions

You can have a personal pension plan (sometimes called a 'self-employed retirement annuity') if you are in non-pensionable employment, or work for yourself, or are in partnership. Being in non-pensionable employment could mean that you are employed by a company with a scheme that you have decided not to join. However, it is important to recognize that you cannot be in a company pension scheme *and* claim tax relief for contributions to a personal pension plan.

Personal pensions are allowed against your highest rates of income tax, normally up to a maximum of 17½ per cent of your net earnings. If you were born before 1934, however, this maximum figure is increased as follows:

Year of birth	% of net earnings allowed for personal premiums
1916–1933	20%
1914–1915	21%
1912–1913	24%
1910–1911	26.5%
Before 1910	29.5%

You can elect for a premium paid in one year to be treated as having been paid in the previous year, or in some cases even one year earlier. Conversely, if you do not pay the maximum premium allowed in any year, unused relief may be carried forward for up to six years.

The benefits provided under personal pension plans tend to

be restricted, for tax purposes, by the amount of the allowable premium, rather than by direct reference to earnings. However, plans are very flexible, and a variety of combinations of personal pension, widow's pension, dependant's pension and lump-sum payments can all be established within the value of the fund created.

Pensions are an extremely technical investment area, and because it is vital that you get it right, we would recommend the services of a specialist pension broker in order to ensure that maximum advantage is taken of tax legislation. Pensions really do present a golden opportunity for investment. As we discussed in the example at the beginning of this chapter, contributions to a pension fund can be made gross, whereas most of the other investments you will make will have to be made from net income.

In addition, pension funds are the only financial bodies other than friendly societies whose activities are entirely tax-free. In other words, all the other activites of, say, an insurance company have their profits taxed – not so pension funds. To put their worth in perspective with other investments, pension funds should achieve a growth of 15 per cent per annum compound, and even that figure does not demonstrate their true worth, because the contributions you make to a pension fund are from gross income. If you were to invest from net income, you would need to achieve a growth of some 22½ per cent per annum compound to obtain the same result. Beat that – if you can!

14 The international marketplace

As you drive your faultlessly efficient Japanese car at a fuel-consumption rate that puts British Leyland to shame, as you bash away on your elegant, high-tech German typewriter, or slip into your beautifully designed tracksuit made in Hong Kong, you may be tempted towards a momentary lack of patriotism. Why, you may ask yourself, am I looking exclusively at the UK market for my investments? Why is my money in sterling instead of dollars or marks? What's all this about cocoa futures, gold, Saudi crude oil and offshore tax havens?

For reasons which we must admit are entirely commercial rather than patriotic, we would suggest that you dismiss any thought of *direct* involvement in international markets – whether it be in currency, securities or commodities. They are too specialist, too speculative and too expensive to deal in, and it is far too risky to trust an overseas agent or financial institution to handle them for you. If you feel strongly about investing in overseas markets, then do so through a unit trust, investment trust or investment bond with a fund aimed at the market in which you are interested. As we have already stated, some of the financial management groups do offer specialist funds linked to a particular industry, a particular country or both. Assuming you choose a bona fide company, you can at least be sure that your investment is being properly looked after, and properly protected. Before making your investment, however, you should examine the company's track record, and have the comfort of knowing that you have a sound base for backing your hunch.

The furthest we could recommend you to go internationally is to one of the offshore currency funds managed by various London merchant banks. This sort of fund is ethically run and carefully controlled – in other words, some of the inherent risks are removed. You can invest a minimum of £1000 (or its currency equivalent) to back the management skill and judgement of the experts in the money market. This will be attractive to you if you feel that capital profits are now to be made by dealing in currency. Nevertheless, we must point out the volatile and speculative nature of these funds in today's market conditions.

We are honestly not being stick-in-the-mud about this – just sensible. We want your money to work for you, not disappear in a puff of smoke.

Section 3   The External Factors

We have examined the numerous opportunities available to you for investing your money. Now is the time to look at the external factors that may influence your decision. These fall into two very distinct categories. On the one hand, we are looking at the advisers and agents you may be tempted to use to help you with your investment decision; on the other, we are looking at the events that can happen in the world, which are quite beyond your control, but which may equally influence your thinking.

15   The advisers

We would like to feel that, having read our book thus far, you have a fairly clear idea of the sort of investment planning you wish to make, and this being the case, it is simply a question of going to the appropriate adviser to help you implement your plan. If you wish to buy a house, then you will go to an estate agent to help you find one and to a solicitor to arrange the purchase for you. If you want to buy shares, then you will go to a stockbroker; for life assurance, to an insurance broker and so on. This is the way in which you should approach advisers – after *you* have decided what *you* want to do, you should go to them to help you achieve your plan in the best possible way. Of course, we are not suggesting that you should be impervious to their advice and guidance, but our experience would suggest that most advisers respond better to instructions than to woolly requests for advice. Let's look at the various advisers associated with investment.

Stockbrokers

There are over 200 Stock Exchange member firms from which to choose, but on the whole, small London firms and provincial firms provide the modest investor with the best personal service. Essentially, a stockbroker will deal on your behalf, however small your portfolio, but if you are seeking his advice and backup services, you need to recognize that, unless you are a fairly substantial investor, you are not going to generate much interest from him. This is not intended to be a criticism of

stockbrokers – it is simply not worth their while spending a great deal of time on someone with just a few thousand pounds to invest.

Having said that, it is important to try and establish some sort of personal rapport with your stockbroker, however small your investment. How do you find one? Personal recommendation is clearly the best method. If you know no one who uses a stockbroker, ask your bank, your solicitor or your accountant to recommend someone.

The Stock Exchange motto – 'My word is my bond' – is still the basis upon which instructions are made and acted upon between broker and client. Whether your verbal instructions are to buy £500 worth of shares or sell a quarter of a million, your stockbroker must have faith in you, and you in him. On a mundane level, brokers will require bank references before they begin dealing for you, and you, in turn, will need to provide them with the personal audit described in Chapter 2, so that they can have a full understanding of your financial position. Do not be tempted to enhance the information you give – tell them everything about yourself. Remember, it is trust you are trying to establish.

Once you have identified the firm you are going to use, the next step is to organize a meeting to see the broker of your choice and discuss both your requirements and his/her recommendations. One of the questions brokers will ask is whether you wish them to act on a *discretionary*, or *consultative*, basis. This means they need to know whether you wish to be responsible for day-to-day decisions on your portfolio, or whether you would like them to handle these for you. There are degrees of discretionary power: you might tell your broker that you are happy for him to act on your behalf up to a certain figure or in a specific market sector, or you may wish him to consult you on every decision, so that he only acts on your specific instructions. On the whole, brokers are not over-anxious for a discretionary brief on a small investment, since it does not make commercial sense to be constantly reviewing a small portfolio – either for you or for them. They cannot justify the time, nor you the costs of constantly changing your investments.

This brings us to the question of brokerage fees. A stockbroker's fee for buying and selling shares is set by the Stock Exchange at 1.65 per cent (plus VAT) of the value of the shares involved, but costs can amount to more than this if minimum charges are applied to small transactions. Most brokers charge a minimum of £15 per transaction, though some large firms of brokers will charge as much as £25 per transaction.

As a result of the meeting with your stockbroker, you will decide on which investments you are going to make. The following day, you will receive a call from your broker, telling you what he has bought and at precisely what price. You will then be sent contract notes for each of your purchases. Each note shows the number of shares purchased, at what price and the total price. It will also show the stamp duty payable and the brokerage fee. Also indicated on the contract note will be the settlement date – i.e. the date on which you have to pay for your shares. There are two settlement dates each month, so it is likely that you will have to pay for your shares within two weeks of receiving the contract note.

A few weeks after your purchase, you will receive a share certificate direct from the company in which you have invested, and this will signify a change of relationship: now that you are a shareholder, you will deal direct with the company, rather than through your broker. The company will send you dividends, usually every six months, and with each dividend payment, you will receive a voucher showing the amount of the payment and the tax deduction. You are also entitled to see the annual accounts of the company, which will be sent to you automatically, and to attend the annual general meeting.

As and when you wish to sell your shares, the reverse procedure applies. You instruct your broker, giving him the minimum price at which you are prepared to sell your shares, and he will telephone you once he has achieved a sale. You will then be sent a contract note, with a settlement date, but on this occasion it is the date on which your broker will pay you.

So, having established how stockbrokers operate, what faith should you have in their advice? There are considerably conflicting views on this. We have a friend who declares firmly that he listens very carefully to the advice given to him by his stockbroker, and then does exactly the opposite. This, he claims, ensures successful investment! Seriously, it does need to be recognized that stockbrokers, like everyone else, get it wrong sometimes, but they do have direct access to detailed information on the companies involved, and they have experience and a feel for the market. Their main fault, perhaps, is a tendency to say *no* a little too infrequently – in other words, they should be more heavy-handed in advising you against certain investments.

It should be remembered that stockbrokers not only deal with stocks and shares, but also with the buying and selling of gilts, unit trusts and investment trusts.

Investment consultants

There is a growing market for selling financial packages aimed at providing all of an individual's needs, and this is what an investment consultant aims to do. The problem is that, all too often, they are linked, by way of substantial up-front commission, to a large organization such as an insurance company or an investment trust. While it is probably going too far to say that this colours their judgement, it certainly gives them a rather blinkered view. You cannot get away from the fact that the average investment consultant's immediate reward for allegedly solving your financial problems is a commission, and undoubtedly he or she will push your thinking towards the company or companies who will provide him or her with that commission. Perhaps this is a somewhat cavalier attitude, but having read our book, we do not think you need an investment consultant; we think you should be dealing directly with the people who are actually going to be *doing* something for you.

Insurance/pension brokers

Insurance brokers act on commission, but unlike investment consultants, they receive a commission from every single insurance company they deal with and this means that their advice will be entirely impartial. Insurance brokers cost nothing. They are acting as agents for the insurance companies and are paid by them. This does not mean that insurance companies will load your premiums to pay the broker's commission, nor indeed that you will get a better deal if you go to the companies direct.

For the purposes of investment, you do want to choose your insurance broker carefully because you are looking for a firm that specializes in life assurance and pensions. Particularly in the provinces, there are a number of very small insurance brokers who are amply qualified to sort out the best possible deal for car insurance, but cannot adequately advise you on life assurance or pensions. So look for a specialist – ask your bank, accountant or solicitor for a recommendation.

Unlike stockbrokers, the good thing about insurance brokers is that you will receive the same standard of care and attention whether you are looking to place £500 or £50,000. Insurance brokers are used to dealing with small investors and are well aware that they owe their livelihoods to them. Try and find a broker you like and instinctively trust; you will find it a very worthwhile relationship.

Banks

As we have already indicated in Chapter 5, we believe that banks are best suited to the handling of money, rather than the doling out of financial advice. If you do decide to seek your bank's advice, please use the facilities of their specialist departments, rather than relying on the views of one individual manager.

On a more mundane level, banks are very useful sources of information. Certainly your bank manager will be able to put you in touch with a good accountant, solicitor, insurance broker and stockbroker, and he or she will also be able to provide you with a wealth of information as to the various types of available unit trusts, investment trusts, life assurance schemes and so on. So look on banks more as excellent places for gathering information, rather than as serious investment advisers.

Accountants

The accountant's forte is, without doubt, taxation. No one knows as much about taxation as an accountant, and since tax is a fundamental part of overall investment thinking, accountants can be extremely useful in handing out general investment advice. Accountants are trained to be cautious, and while the advice you receive may not be flamboyant, it is likely to be sound, provided you deal with a chartered accountant who specializes in personal investment and taxation affairs.

Again, though, unless your affairs are very complicated we would tend to suggest that you first go shopping for your particular investment requirement and then, before signing anything, take it to an accountant to discuss the tax implications. Accountants react better to giving advice on specific proposals, rather than dealing in hypotheses. Certainly never sign yourself up for any major investment plan without first seeking the view of an independent accountant.

Solicitors

We do not really see solicitors as investment advisers. If you are buying or selling a house or if you are making your will, use a solicitor. If you are setting up a trust fund or covenant, then having a solicitor not only to advise you but perhaps act as a trustee is very useful. However, detailed financial planning is not really their field. While this statement will probably bring the Law Society crashing round our ears, it is our opinion that solicitors are not as experienced in taxation matters as accountants.

The media

Our eleven-year-old daughter Lucy sauntered into our bedroom the other morning and announced that she would like to buy shares in The Really Useful Company – Andrew Lloyd-Webber's production company, which has been responsible for such musical masterpieces as *Cats*. This clearly demonstrates the power and influence of the media, for even a few years ago, share buying would never have occurred to an eleven-year-old. Think of the hype given to the British Telecom shares, which must have made the entire British nation aware of what was happening on the stock market.

The media probably provide most of us with our daily knowledge and feel of financial affairs – on television, on the radio and, possibly the most influential of all, in the newspapers. The times we live in have tended to encourage this interest. The Conservative government's programme of privatization of nationalized industries has made people more aware of stocks and shares. Increasing unemployment has provided more people with a lump sum redundancy payment as well as the time to wonder what to do with it. The rapid increase in the number of small businesses has produced a spate of books and articles on how to manage money, and changes within the family have contributed to the need for more knowledge as well. The days when mothers stayed at home with the kids while fathers went out to work are long gone, and the range of relationships and family circumstances that now prevail varies hugely, demanding more inventive investment planning.

Radio and television are useful, but we feel that when it comes to financial advice, the written word is king. The 'heavy' establishment newspapers provide good, sound advice, although it is sometimes difficult to get at it, and most of the articles assume that the reader has a working knowledge of the City and its affairs. The more sensational tabloids are hopeless, though some of the less lurid ones do have some very good money pages, usually on a weekly basis. However, without doubt, we consider that the specialist money and financial magazines are by far the most useful to the first-time investor. Go to a major newsagent and simply look along the shelves: you will find a number of really useful publications, offering wide-ranging advice.

There are also a number of tip sheets available (usually on subscription), aimed at giving you the latest stock market advice hot off the press. On the whole, we would not recommend these unless, of course, you find them genuinely interesting.

So what have we got in terms of advisers – indeed, what advice can we give you on advisers? On balance, avoid the general advisers and use those most appropriate to your particular requirements. Do not be intimidated or bullied by the more imposing of them. If they use jargon you do not understand, ask them to explain again in plain English. Question and query until you fully understand what they are saying. It does not matter if they think you are overcautious – it is not their money and their lives that are at stake, but *yours*. And when you have listened to all the advice they can give you, sign nothing. Go away to somewhere quiet and think about everything they have said and everything that you want your money to do for you and your family. Then make your decision, using the best adviser you will ever have – your own good sense.

16   The world about us

Investment decisions and saving plans cannot be made sensibly without taking some sort of view of the economic environment in which we live and the world about us.

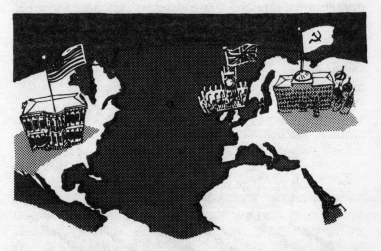

So many factors affect the economy and, in turn, affect us and our investments. The UK economy is influenced not only by our own government policy, but by the stability of the international political scene as a whole. There are so many elements to take into account – the long-term effect of the growth of the new industrial nations, the Eastern bloc and the Third World, the performance of Europe and the United States, unemployment and the specific performance of certain key industries. All these factors will influence the value of the money in your pocket, the value of your property, your job prospects, inflation, interest rates and the performance of the Stock Exchange – now and in five and twenty years' time.

This is not the place for a lecture on world politics, nor on the ebb and flow of the world money market, but it is important that, while these factors may be outside your control, you are none the less aware of their existence. Let's look at what has happened in the last few years.

The major influence on world economy in recent times has been the sudden and sharp rise in oil prices, which produced enormous problems for the industrial nations. Without doubt, oil prices triggered off the recession and the high rates of interest, which, mercifully, seem now to have receded. Today, economies throughout the world are on the up and up. Stock markets are a measure of confidence in the future and are at record levels. Interest rates continue to come down, which in turn fuels industrial growth. Even inflation appears to have been kept at a very low level.

However, in the UK, we still have a legacy of problems, not the least of which is the three to four million people who are unemployed. Equally fundamental is the state of our manufacturing industries – old industries, many of which are now outdated. Will they recover, or drift on and die as new nations take up the mantle of industry and production? For this reason particularly, it is necessary to look carefully, not just at the economy as a whole, but at individual market sectors. Take one example. Up until 1985, the electronics sector was riding high in this country. Electronic shares were growth shares, highly valued with very low yields. Suddenly, as new nations began to produce better, cheaper products, problems developed. Profits began falling, the image was dented and shares fell dramatically – and they are still droopy, despite the high level of the stock market generally.

When the stock market climbs to record levels, after a time it always turns down, if only temporarily, before climbing again. Despite all the sophistication of the analysts, the chart watchers and their computers, the peaks and troughs of the stock market are still basically unpredictable. However, whether you are investing in stocks and shares or not, the stock market is still an excellent yardstick for measuring the state of the economy. The market represents the big investors' measure of confidence, and as such, it anticipates situations. If fund managers, bankers and brokers begin to feel that next year might see a slowdown in the economy, then the market will drop – not next year, but *now*. Watch it carefully, for it represents the trend of the future.

Section 4   Case Histories

Casebook report no. 1

NAME: Timothy Johnson (purchasing manager) AGE: 48

SPOUSE'S NAME: Jennifer Johnson (secretary) AGE: 44

CHILDREN/GRANDCHILDREN/DEPENDANTS: 3 daughters – aged 21, 19 and 16

HEALTH OF FAMILY: Good

GROSS INCOME: SELF: £21,000   SPOUSE: £6000 (anticipated)

HOME OWNER (VALUE): £75,000   SIZE OF MORTGAGE: £12,000

PENSION ARRANGEMENTS: Company pension scheme (non contributory)

OTHER EXISTING INVESTMENT/SAVINGS: £1500 (approx. on bank deposit), £500 premium bonds

AMOUNT AVAILABLE TO SAVE/INVEST IN ADDITION TO THE ABOVE: (A) ANNUALLY: £4000–5000 (B) LUMP SUM: £—

SPECIAL CIRCUMSTANCES: Our two elder daughters have left home and the youngest is taking her 'O' levels this summer. My wife has decided to take up working again and has been offered a secretarial job at £6000 p.a.

OBJECTIVES: Rather than squander this extra income, we would like to invest it for our old age. Assuming my wife receives approx. £4500 after tax, we have agreed that I should contribute £3000 and she £1000 to some sort of saving plan. What do you suggest?

We think you and Jennifer should treat your two savings contributions quite separately.

In your case, we would suggest you use the £3000 p.a. to top up your existing pension arrangements. This is by far the most effective way of saving for your old age.

In Jennifer's case, we would suggest she places her £1000 either in unit trusts with a high growth and low yield, or in a National Savings plan. Either way, look on her investment as a five-year plan only. By then your youngest daughter will be off your hands, and you might decide to use some of the money for a really good holiday. Alternatively, if all three daughters decide to marry in the same year, you might need every penny!

Casebook report no. 2

NAME: Mary Henderson (shop assistant) AGE: 21

SPOUSE'S NAME: Chris Henderson (car mechanic) AGE: 22

CHILDREN/GRANDCHILDREN/DEPENDANTS: Expecting first baby

HEALTH OF FAMILY: Excellent

GROSS INCOME: SELF: £4000   SPOUSE: £6000

HOME OWNER (VALUE): £—   SIZE OF MORTGAGE: £—

PENSION ARRANGEMENTS: None

OTHER EXISTING INVESTMENT/SAVINGS: None

AMOUNT AVAILABLE TO SAVE/INVEST IN ADDITION TO THE
ABOVE: (A) ANNUALLY: £—   (B) LUMP SUM: £—

SPECIAL CIRCUMSTANCES: Chris and I live in a rented flat that
costs us £200 per month. We were hoping to save for a place of
our own, but now I am pregnant and will have to give up work,
we will never be able to do it.

OBJECTIVES: To have our own home. We are close to my Mum
and Dad who live just up the road – they would help us if they
could but they have no spare cash themselves.

You can have your own home, but only if you are prepared to make sacrifices now. If your parents are prepared to help, this is what you must do.

(1) Give up your flat immediately and move in with your parents, thus saving £200 per month.

(2) Open a building society account and begin saving every penny you can lay your hands on.

(3) Begin looking at the cheapest possible freehold property in your area. Forget your dream house – concentrate on value for money.

(4) Do your sums. Assuming the building society will give you a 95–100 per cent mortgage, work out how much you can spend on a house and still meet the mortgage repayments on Chris's salary.

(5) Whilst your parents cannot give you cash, could they give you a guarantee for the amount of the deposit?

All this will mean tremendous hardship initially, but it is worth it to get on the first rung of the property ladder. It is also the only way you and Chris can build up any wealth at this stage in your lives. Whatever you do, though, do not take on a bigger mortgage than you can afford.

Casebook report no. 3

NAME: Magnus J. Grant (actor) AGE: 40

SPOUSE'S NAME: Hilary Grant (teacher) AGE: 41

CHILDREN/GRANDCHILDREN/DEPENDANTS: 2 sons – aged 11 and 13

HEALTH OF FAMILY: Good

GROSS INCOME: SELF: £70,000 (approx.) SPOUSE: £3000

HOME OWNER (VALUE): £80,000   SIZE OF MORTGAGE: £30,000

PENSION ARRANGEMENTS: None

OTHER EXISTING INVESTMENT/SAVINGS: Quoted shares £10,000

AMOUNT AVAILABLE TO SAVE/INVEST IN ADDITION TO THE ABOVE: (A) ANNUALLY: £20,000   (B) LUMP SUM: £—

SPECIAL CIRCUMSTANCES: At present I am very fortunate, with a lot of television and stage work, which produces high income. I cannot rely on this continuing. I can easily be out of work for months at a time.

OBJECTIVES: (1) Avoid some tax on present earnings if possible. (2) Put something aside for a rainy day.

We suggest that *if* you are prepared to take a twenty-year view, most of your available surplus should go into a personal pension plan. Almost certainly, a single premium of £20,000 would be wholly allowed for tax (partly spread back into previous years). This could actually save you up to £12,000 of high-rate income tax.

Knowing that you will be saving that tax, you might feel that you can invest a further £10,000. We suggest that sum should be put into investment bonds – partly with general equity funds and partly with overseas equity funds.

You will need to keep some money readily available to meet annual tax bills. Short gilts would be useful for that purpose.

Casebook report no. 4

NAME: Dorothy Brant AGE: 66

SPOUSE'S NAME: — AGE: —

CHILDREN/GRANDCHILDREN/DEPENDANTS: None

HEALTH OF FAMILY: I am in good health.

GROSS INCOME: SELF: £2000   SPOUSE: £—

HOME OWNER (VALUE): £75,000   SIZE OF MORTGAGE: Nil

PENSION ARRANGEMENTS: OAP

OTHER EXISTING INVESTMENT/SAVINGS: None

AMOUNT AVAILABLE TO SAVE/INVEST IN ADDITION TO THE
ABOVE: (A) ANNUALLY: £—   (B) LUMP SUM: £—

SPECIAL CIRCUMSTANCES: I have looked after my invalid father
for many years. He has recently died. His pension died with
him. I have the big family home and the contents, but no
capital.

OBJECTIVES: I need income, and security for the future.

We think you have two alternatives, Dorothy, and the choice is a very personal one, which only you can make. Obviously, taking a long-term view you need a much smaller, more compact home. We suggest either:

(1) borrow whatever is necessary – £5000/£10,000/£15,000 – and divide your large house into two completely self-contained homes, one for you and one to let. This will give you extra income of at least £3000 a year *after* paying the mortgage interest. You will find a building society to lend you the money on an 'interest only' basis – with no capital repayment required. Your income will be inflation proof if you grant a lease with regular rent reviews.

or

(2) sell your present house and buy a much smaller home for, say, £35,000–£40,000. Invest half the capital you then have in National Savings income bonds and half in a general equity fund unit trust. In five or ten years' time, consider cashing the investments and buying an annuity.

Casebook report no. 5

NAME: Thomas Mackenzie (store manager) AGE: 41

SPOUSE'S NAME: Juliet Mackenzie (not working) AGE: 37

CHILDREN/GRANDCHILDREN/DEPENDANTS: 2 children, aged 4 and 8

HEALTH OF FAMILY: Good

GROSS INCOME: SELF: £18,000   SPOUSE: £—

HOME OWNER (VALUE): £50,000   SIZE OF MORTGAGE: £20,000

PENSION ARRANGEMENTS: Company pension scheme (non contributory)

OTHER EXISTING INVESTMENT/SAVINGS: £2000 in National Savings certificates, £20 premium bonds

AMOUNT AVAILABLE TO SAVE/INVEST IN ADDITION TO THE ABOVE: (A) ANNUALLY: £—   (B) LUMP SUM: £90,000

SPECIAL CIRCUMSTANCES: My mother has just died, leaving me her house which I find is valued at £90,000, including contents.

OBJECTIVES: To invest the money received from the sale of the house wisely for the benefit of my family.

By the time you have paid inheritance tax and the costs of sale, let's assume you have £80,000 to invest.

Firstly, we would recommend that you consider buying a bigger house with the maximum tax-effective mortgage. Think in terms of a house costing £80,000 – paid for by £30,000 from the sale of your present house, £30,000 mortgage and £20,000 from your inheritance.

Secondly, assume you will spend £10,000 on your new home.

Thirdly, use £20,000 to invest in National Savings or gilts for security and capital growth, £20,000 to top up your pension and £20,000 on a higher-risk investment: the stock market if it appeals to you; if not, try investment bonds.

That leaves just £5000. Take Juliet and the children on a really super holiday and do not forget to raise a glass to good old Mum.

Casebook report no. 6

NAME: Veronica Miller (publishing editor) AGE: 26

BOYFRIEND'S NAME: Antony Blackburn (writer) AGE: 37

CHILDREN/GRANDCHILDREN/DEPENDANTS: None

HEALTH OF FAMILY: Excellent

GROSS INCOME: SELF: £17,000 BOYFRIEND: £21,000 on average

BOYFRIEND'S HOME (VALUE): £55,000
SIZE OF MORTGAGE: £30,000

PENSION ARRANGEMENTS: I have a company pension scheme;
Antony has none.

OTHER EXISTING INVESTMENT/SAVINGS: None

AMOUNT AVAILABLE TO SAVE/INVEST IN ADDITION TO THE
ABOVE: (A) ANNUALLY: £— (B) LUMP SUM: £11,000
temporarily

SPECIAL CIRCUMSTANCES: Until recently, my boyfriend and I
both had our own flats in London. Now we want to buy a
cottage together, while still retaining Antony's flat.

OBJECTIVES: I have already sold my flat, which has left me with
£11,000. I want to invest this on a short-term basis while we find
a cottage.

Put your money on three-month deposit with a building society – preferably the one you and Antony will be using to purchase your cottage. There is no point in looking at fancier investments – you must be able to get hold of your money quickly when the right property comes along.

A point to consider: Antony's London flat is clearly his main residence. If the cottage is purchased in your name and you treat it as your main residence, you would both be eligible for mortgage relief—assuming, as your enquiry suggests, that you are not intending to marry at present.

Casebook report no. 7

NAME: Alfred Scott AGE: 65

SPOUSE'S NAME: Elizabeth Scott AGE: 62

CHILDREN/GRANDCHILDREN/DEPENDANTS: Married daughter and two grand-daughters, aged 2 and 4

HEALTH OF FAMILY: Good

GROSS INCOME: SELF: £11,000   SPOUSE: £2000

HOME OWNER (VALUE): £70,000   SIZE OF MORTGAGE: Nil

PENSION ARRANGEMENTS: Receiving company pension and OAP.

OTHER EXISTING INVESTMENT/SAVINGS: £25,000 in National Savings and unit trusts

AMOUNT AVAILABLE TO SAVE/INVEST IN ADDITION TO THE ABOVE: (A) ANNUALLY: £(see below)   (B) LUMP SUM: £(see below)

SPECIAL CIRCUMSTANCES: We live quite modestly and well within our means.

OBJECTIVES: Would like to do something for our grandchildren.

On the facts you have given, your earnings are too high for you to receive age allowance, so we work out that your tax bill is about £2700, and your net income is therefore £10,300 a year.

We recommend you enter into a covenant for £2000 a year to each of the girls. This will cost you £4000 less tax @ 29% – i.e. £2840 a year. But because your income is reduced by the covenants, you should now be entitled to age allowance, so this will reduce your tax by nearly £250 a year, and the net cost of the covenants is therefore £2590. You might have difficulty persuading your tax inspector to allow age relief, because the wording of the appropriate legislation is unclear. In our view, the covenants should reduce income for this purpose, although we have been unable to get a positive ruling from Somerset House to this effect.

Your daughter will reclaim the whole of the tax deducted, and the children will therefore actually receive the full £4000. Depending on future plans for schooling, this could be invested in educational policies or, alternatively, investment bonds.

Casebook report no. 8

NAME: Jean Forbes (bookkeeper) AGE: 38

SPOUSE'S NAME: — AGE:—

CHILDREN/GRANDCHILDREN/DEPENDANTS: None

HEALTH OF FAMILY: I am in good health.

GROSS INCOME: SELF: £7000   SPOUSE: £—

HOME OWNER (VALUE): £60,000   SIZE OF MORTGAGE: Nil

PENSION ARRANGEMENTS: None

OTHER EXISTING INVESTMENT/SAVINGS: See below

AMOUNT AVAILABLE TO SAVE/INVEST IN ADDITION TO THE
ABOVE: (A) ANNUALLY: £—   (B) LUMP SUM: £100,000

SPECIAL CIRCUMSTANCES: My husband died last month after a
car crash. It seems that the mortgage has been settled and I
could get about £100,000 from life policies.

OBJECTIVES: I don't know what to do. We were only married
three years ago, and I feel that I am not even entitled to this
huge amount of money.

Our first advice, Jean, is to make no long-term arrangements or commitments for at least a year, possibly longer. Your whole world has been turned upside down, and you cannot make any sensible investment plans until things settle down and you know what the future has in store. Things *will* look brighter than they do today.

You don't tell us anything about your family or your husband's family – for example, do you both have elderly parents? You might consider a gift of a few thousand pounds to each of them in a few months' time.

In the meantime, go for *secure* investments – don't worry about inflation for the next year or so. Don't try and get high income. Split your available funds equally among National Savings deposit bonds, a long-notice building society account and a three-month notice bank deposit, and review the whole position in a year's time.

Casebook report no. 9

NAME: David Lane (copywriter) AGE: 34

SPOUSE'S NAME: Gill Lane (computer analyst) AGE: 38

CHILDREN/GRANDCHILDREN/DEPENDANTS: None

HEALTH OF FAMILY: Good

GROSS INCOME: SELF: £14,000   SPOUSE: £20,000

HOME OWNER (VALUE): £85,000   SIZE OF MORTGAGE: £30,000

PENSION ARRANGEMENTS: Company schemes

OTHER EXISTING INVESTMENT/SAVINGS: None

AMOUNT AVAILABLE TO SAVE/INVEST IN ADDITION TO THE
ABOVE: (A) ANNUALLY: £750   (B) LUMP SUM: £—

SPECIAL CIRCUMSTANCES: I have finally given up smoking and
am therefore saving £15 per week.

OBJECTIVES: To invest this money in something positive to
make sure I really do kick the habit!

What a good idea! Here are our suggestions:

Invest £100 p.a. in a friendly society investment bond, which will virtually double your investment in ten years, giving you a nest egg of approximately £2000.

Invest £50 p.a. in premium bonds – well, why not? It has to be worth the gamble!

Finally, invest £600 p.a. in a building society subscription share account. This will earn you (at today's rates) approximately 7% (net of tax) and is easy to get at. This is really the point – you need to set yourself a target so that when your building society savings reach, say, £2000, you have a wonderful holiday, a new car or whatever may be your heart's desire. This thought will hopefully sustain you every time you are tempted to reach for the dreadful weed!

Casebook report no. 10

NAME: Angela Hobday AGE: 32

SPOUSE'S NAME: (divorced) AGE:—

CHILDREN/GRANDCHILDREN/DEPENDANTS: 1 son aged 7 (Mark David Hobday)

HEALTH OF FAMILY: Self/son both first class

GROSS INCOME: SELF: £15,000   SPOUSE: £—

HOME OWNER (VALUE): £25,000   SIZE OF MORTGAGE: £23,000

PENSION ARRANGEMENTS: None

OTHER EXISTING INVESTMENT/SAVINGS: None

AMOUNT AVAILABLE TO SAVE/INVEST IN ADDITION TO THE ABOVE: (A) ANNUALLY: £500   (B) LUMP SUM: £—

SPECIAL CIRCUMSTANCES: I am a single parent, with a full-time demanding job, small son and a part-time mother's help – not much spare cash.

OBJECTIVES: I am worried about Mark in case anything happens to me. His father has remarried and lives in Argentina. What can I do?

INVESTMENT AND SAVINGS ADVICE

For immediate peace of mind, we suggest you look first at your insurance arrangements. Presumably you have a mortgage protection policy that would pay off the loan should you die. Make sure the house and contents and car insurance are all *more* than adequate. Take out permanent health insurance in case you become ill or disabled. You are obviously holding down a good job – ask your employer to cover you for sickness under a BUPA or PPP scheme (it's in their interest as well as yours).

Then take out a whole life policy for £100,000, in favour of Mark. A ten- or fifteen-year term policy will be the cheapest, and that will provide security during his critical school days.

Finally we recommend you subscribe £100 a year for a friendly society baby bond (investment bond). That will give Mark quite a reasonable nest egg in his early twenties.

Casebook report no. 11

NAME: Joan Rigby AGE: 72

SPOUSE'S NAME: George Rigby AGE: 78

CHILDREN/GRANDCHILDREN/DEPENDANTS: Married son and 1 grand-daughter aged 13

HEALTH OF FAMILY: I am very fit but my husband is only fair.

GROSS INCOME: SELF: £8000 (joint)

HOME OWNER (VALUE): £90,000   SIZE OF MORTGAGE: Nil

PENSION ARRANGEMENTS: My husband receives a company pension worth £4500. I will continue to receive £3000 if he dies.

OTHER EXISTING INVESTMENT/SAVINGS: We have various National Savings accounts and high-income unit trusts – total £3000.

AMOUNT AVAILABLE TO SAVE/INVEST IN ADDITION TO THE ABOVE: (A) ANNUALLY: £—   (B) LUMP SUM: £—

SPECIAL CIRCUMSTANCES: If my husband dies before me, I will move into a smaller house or flat.

OBJECTIVES: We would like a little more income and some spending money for one or two more good holidays – should I cash in my savings?

There is no need to use your savings.

We suggest you take a £30,000 mortgage and invest £27,000 of the loan on the purchase of an annuity on your joint lives. The annuity would produce additional income (after tax) of £2500. The interest would be allowed for tax, and would cost (net) £1800. So you would have an extra £3000 in the bank, and additional net income of £700 a year.

If you move in a few years to a smaller home, you can pay off the mortgage, so your net income will increase at that time by that £1800, which will make up for the drop in your pension that will occur then.

Casebook report no. 12

NAME: Derek Parsons (advertising executive) AGE: 34

SPOUSE'S NAME: — AGE: —

CHILDREN/GRANDCHILDREN/DEPENDANTS: None – single – but have 2 Siamese cats.

HEALTH OF FAMILY: I am in amazingly good health.

GROSS INCOME: SELF: £25,000 SPOUSE: £—

HOME OWNER (VALUE): £35,000 SIZE OF MORTGAGE: £15,000

PENSION ARRANGEMENTS: Good company pension scheme

OTHER EXISTING INVESTMENT/SAVINGS: None

AMOUNT AVAILABLE TO SAVE/INVEST IN ADDITION TO THE ABOVE: (A) ANNUALLY: £5000 (B) LUMP SUM: £—

SPECIAL CIRCUMSTANCES: I am a bachelor – well paid and in an exciting job with a go-ahead company. I have lots of holidays and travel.

OBJECTIVES: I aim to settle down a bit and put something aside for the future.

Clearly the National Savings Bank is not for you! We suggest:

(1) Invest as much as you can in 'bricks and mortar'. Sell your present house and buy another in the £55/60,000 bracket with a £40,000 mortgage. Make absolutely sure the location is right. The growth in your salary will pay for the extra mortgage.

(2) Invest your £5000 a year (which we assume is surplus income) in stocks and shares. You have obviously got business acumen, so do it yourself. Buy the *Financial Times* every day and also get a selection of investment magazines regularly so you really understand the markets.

Make sure that you take advantage of the £2400 a year tax-free investment allowed under the Personal Equity Plan.

Have a go!

Casebook report no. 13

NAME: Mrs A. Baker AGE: 66

SPOUSE'S NAME: — AGE: —

CHILDREN/GRANDCHILDREN/DEPENDANTS: Married son in New Zealand, married daughter lives a few miles away.

HEALTH OF FAMILY: I am in good health.

GROSS INCOME: SELF: £660 + OAP SPOUSE: £—

HOME OWNER (VALUE): £35,000 SIZE OF MORTGAGE: Nil

PENSION ARRANGEMENTS: None

OTHER EXISTING INVESTMENT/SAVINGS: £6000 in building society since husband died; £1000 National Savings certificates; £100 premium bonds.

AMOUNT AVAILABLE TO SAVE/INVEST IN ADDITION TO THE ABOVE: (A) ANNUALLY: £— (B) LUMP SUM: £—

SPECIAL CIRCUMSTANCES: Will go to live with daughter in a few years' time, although she hasn't got much room. My husband died 4 years ago.

OBJECTIVES: Would like to live a bit more comfortably and feel more settled about the future.

With your income, Mrs Baker, you are not liable for any tax, but you are paying tax on your building society account.

Transfer the whole £6000 to an investment account with the National Savings Bank. They will pay you gross interest, and you will actually receive £4.50 a week more. If you need a little extra cash from time to time – cash a few of your National Savings certificates.

Why not suggest to your daughter and her husband that they look round for a slightly larger house with separate granny flat? You could give them £20,000 towards it from the sale of your own house, without feeling in any way disloyal to your son in New Zealand.

Casebook report no. 14

NAME: John Skindle (partner in scaffolding business) AGE: 30

SPOUSE'S NAME: — AGE: —

CHILDREN/GRANDCHILDREN/DEPENDANTS: None

HEALTH OF FAMILY: A1

GROSS INCOME: SELF: £50/60,000 SPOUSE: £—

HOME OWNER (VALUE): £— SIZE OF MORTGAGE: £—

PENSION ARRANGEMENTS: None

OTHER EXISTING INVESTMENT/SAVINGS: Own business

AMOUNT AVAILABLE TO SAVE/INVEST IN ADDITION TO THE
ABOVE: (A) ANNUALLY: £— (B) LUMP SUM: £—

SPECIAL CIRCUMSTANCES: Up until now, my partner and I have
made reasonable profits, but this year we will make over
£100,000.

OBJECTIVES: I think I should invest £40,000 in a Business Expansion Scheme. A friend has a company in the building trade,
and he seems to need the money. What do you think?

Don't put money into a friend's business just because of that relationship. Only invest if you believe in the growth of the business. Think carefully about how you will be able to realize your investment after five years.

If you are convinced that you do not require the cash in your own business, why not at least limit your BES investment to £15/20,000, and split the balance between a personal pension plan and a capital growth investment bond?

Casebook report no. 15

NAME: Gordon Hancock (production director) AGE: 45

SPOUSE'S NAME: Judith Hancock (anaesthetist) AGE: 42

CHILDREN/GRANDCHILDREN/DEPENDANTS: 1 daughter, aged 15; 1 son, aged 10.

HEALTH OF FAMILY: Good

GROSS INCOME SELF: £20,000   SPOUSE: £11,000

HOME OWNER (VALUE): £50,000   SIZE OF MORTGAGE: £30,000

PENSION ARRANGEMENTS: None

OTHER EXISTING INVESTMENT/SAVINGS: None; overdraft of £25,000.

AMOUNT AVAILABLE TO SAVE/INVEST IN ADDITION TO THE ABOVE: (A) ANNUALLY: £—   (B) LUMP SUM: £—

SPECIAL CIRCUMSTANCES: I was made redundant five years ago, and started my own business. It was not successful, and I lost all my money. The bank was very good but I still have an overdraft of £25,000. I have a new job with a good solid local company, where my position is secure.

OBJECTIVES: I want to put my overdraft on to a more solid footing. I will repay it, but it is going to take me some time.

We suggest that you set up two separate personal pension plans – one for you and one for Judith. Each should be in the form of a retirement annuity policy with a recognized life assurance company, and should be designed to produce a pension at normal retirement date *plus* a cash sum of £12,500. You should also take out two twenty-year term life assurance policies of £12,500 each.

Since you obviously have a good relationship with your bank, they will undoubtedly grant you two loan accounts of £12,500, each fixed (with interest only) for twenty years. They will require a second mortgage on your house and a charge on the two life assurance policies, and will accept a deposit of the two pension policies (you cannot charge them to the bank) as evidence that the loan is secure and will be repaid.

The premiums for the four policies will total about £1200 a year, but will be all allowed for tax against your income, so the net cost will be about £850. In addition, you will have the interest to pay, but you are paying that anyway.

CONCLUSION

Throughout this book, it has been necessary to generalize in order to cover the many areas of savings and investment, and to anticipate both the opportunities and difficulties with which you may be presented. In an attempt to overcome this, we have included a series of case histories, which demonstrate, on an individual basis, a variety of situations, some of which you may well be facing. We hope these have proved helpful and that you were able to identify with at least some of them.

It may be that, having read this book, you feel that the investments you currently hold are wrong and that you need to make substantial alterations. It could be that you have no investment plan at all – and no savings either, come to that. Whatever your circumstances, if you are approaching a new investment or saving plan, take your time and get it right, for if there is one message we would like to put across more strongly than any other, it is this: investment and savings is not a short-term business or a way to 'get rich quick'. Once a decision has been made, any alteration in the plan usually proves enormously expensive.

Return to those three major factors we discussed at the beginning of the book, which we call *The Three Ts* – TIME, TAX and TEMPERAMENT. Study any investment proposal against the background of these considerations and you will not go far wrong. Good luck!

Alan and Deborah Fowler

Appendix

A glossary of Stock Exchange terms

Account   A Stock Exchange dealing period – normally two, sometimes three weeks. Purchases and sales transacted for the account are due for payment on settlement day, which is the Monday ten days after the account closes.

Bear   Someone who feels that the price of a share, or the market generally, will fall. A bear will sell shares ahead of the anticipated fall – even if he/she does not own them – on the basis that they can be bought later at lower prices, thus making a profit.

Bear Market   A general period of falling share prices.

Blue chips   Ordinary shares in large, first-class companies.

Bonus issue   A free issue of new shares to existing shareholders by the conversion of reserves into share capital. If you have 100 shares worth £10 each and receive a one-for-one bonus issue, you will then have 200 shares. They will still be worth £100 in total, or £5 each. The terms *scrip issue* and *capitalization issue* mean the same thing as bonus issue.

Bull   Someone who feels that the price of a share, or the market generally, will rise. A bull will buy shares ahead of the anticipated rise – even if he/she cannot afford to pay for them – on the basis that he/she can sell them later at a profit.

Bull market   A general period of rising share prices.

Capital distribution   A payment by a company to its shareholders out of capital profits or by way of a reduction in the nominal value of its capital.

Cum div   The term describing a share that is purchased with the entitlement to the next dividend payment.

Dividend A distribution of profit to shareholders – normally twice yearly in the form of an interim dividend and a final dividend. The final dividend is paid when the accounts for the year have been produced and approved by the shareholders. Dividends are paid net of tax (at the current rate of 29 per cent), so a net dividend of £71 is equal to a grossed-up dividend of £100. If you are a non-tax-payer, you can reclaim the tax deducted.

Dividend cover The number of times the total dividend for the year is covered by available earnings of the company after corporation tax and all other charges.

Dividend yield The grossed-up total dividend for the year, per share, expressed as a percentage of the share price. Say you have 1000 shares worth £2 per share and you receive in one year dividends of £71 net of tax. The gross dividend is £100, which is 5 per cent of £2000, and so the dividend yield is 5 per cent.

Earnings The net profit of a company (after corporation tax and all other charges) that is available for distribution to shareholders.

Earnings yield The annual earnings per share attributable to the ordinary shares, expressed as a percentage of the share price. If the dividend described under 'Dividend yield' was twice covered by earnings (a dividend cover of 2), the earnings yield would be 10 per cent.

Ex div The term describing a share that is purchased without the entitlement to the next dividend, which will then be due to the seller, not the buyer.

Growth stock Shares in a company that is performing or is expected to perform at a better rate than the market as a whole.

Market capitalization The total value of a company's ordinary shares at their current price.

Net asset value (per share) The value of the tangible assets of a company, excluding goodwill and after deducting all liabilities and preference capital, expressed as the amount attributable to each ordinary share.

Par value The nominal or face value of a share.

Plc A public limited company as defined by the Companies Act 1980.

150

Rights An entitlement that attaches to a share, giving some sort of preferential right to the holder to subscribe, for instance, to a new issue.

Stag Someone who applies for more shares in a new issue than he/she can afford, in anticipation of being allotted sufficient of them to sell at an immediate profit.